SpringerBriefs in Psychology

SpringerBriefs present concise summaries of cutting-edge research and practical applications across a wide spectrum of fields. Featuring compact volumes of 55 to 125 pages, the series covers a range of content from professional to academic. Typical topics might include:

- A timely report of state-of-the-art analytical techniques
- A bridge between new research results as published in journal articles and a contextual literature review
- A snapshot of a hot or emerging topic
- An in-depth case study or clinical example
- A presentation of core concepts that readers must understand to make independent contributions

SpringerBriefs in Psychology showcase emerging theory, empirical research, and practical application in a wide variety of topics in psychology and related fields. Briefs are characterized by fast, global electronic dissemination, standard publishing contracts, standardized manuscript preparation and formatting guidelines, and expedited production schedules.

Wojciech Kulesza • Dariusz Doliński

Social Biases During Covid 19

Managing the Anxiety of Uncertainty

Springer

Wojciech Kulesza
SWPS University
Warsaw, Poland

Dariusz Doliński
SWPS University
Wroclaw, Poland

ISSN 2192-8363 ISSN 2192-8371 (electronic)
SpringerBriefs in Psychology
ISBN 978-3-031-34705-4 ISBN 978-3-031-34706-1 (eBook)
https://doi.org/10.1007/978-3-031-34706-1

This Springer imprint is published by the registered company Springer Nature Switzerland AG
The registered company address is: Gewerbestrasse 11, 6330 Cham, Switzerland

To our daughters:
Marianna (DD), Hanna (WK), Pola (WK)

Preface

Our fascination with the human psyche and the behaviors emanating from it in situations of mass tragedy and misfortune has invariably accompanied our thoughts for decades. This was determined by fate, since both of us, as inhabitants of Poland, experienced the tragedy of radiation flowing from the destroyed Chernobyl power plant (will we get sick? will we die?), and now through the tragedy of war-stricken Ukraine situated across our eastern border (will we also be affected by the war? how can we help refugees?). Our interests are also professional. The second author of this book, Dariusz Doliński, exactly 35 years ago reported on research into the psychological effects of coping with something deadly, inconceivable, massive, and for which it is impossible to prepare: the explosion at the Chernobyl nuclear power plant. The first author of this monograph, Wojciech Kulesza, as a student of Doliński, wondered – purely hypothetically, of course, because we humans tend to delude ourselves that such a tragedy cannot happen again – about the phenomenon of the human psyche performing incredible mental gymnastics to render a deadly threat bearable. And yet, quite unexpectedly, we have come face to face with such threats again.

COVID-19 and the war in neighboring Ukraine: these are sudden, massive, unpredictable events that – somehow – happened. Memories surfaced, sparking a desire to dust off old research and do novel studies to prepare us for future events. Why? As we know from the wisdom of Malcom X: "The future belongs to those who prepare for it today." Because of how pandemics are becoming the "new normal," and, watching the war in our eastern Slavic sister nation Ukraine, where once again a nuclear power plant is in danger of exploding, we wanted to know more about the present in order to prepare us all for the future.

In the mid-fourteenth century, a disease then known as the Black Death swept through Europe, Africa, and Asia; or, according to the Western-centric beliefs of the time, the entire world. According to various estimates, the Plague, caused by the *Yersinia pestis* bacterium, killed from 25 to as many as 200 million people, which at the time represented from a few percent of the globe's population to nearly half! A more recent, but no less deadly, "Spanish flu," caused by the H1N1 virus, claimed from 50 (e.g., McMillen, 2016; Chrystal, 2021; Pieri, 2021) to as many as a 100 million lives between 1918 and 1919 (e.g., Spinney, 2017). Medical advances and the spread of public health practices ensured that subsequent, later epidemics and pandemics (e.g., Russian flu, avian flu, swine flu, Ebola, polio, HIV/AIDS, or today's well-known COVID-19) did not wreak as much havoc.

Of course, issues related to viruses and bacteria are not the domain of specialists in our field of social science. As social psychologists, we can only express our gratitude to colleagues working in the broader field of medical science for their research, facilitating the creation and dissemination of vaccines and cures. However, we are interested in human behavior that can contribute to both the spread and containment of such diseases and, as research within the Global/Public Health science field shows, such an interdisciplinary approach is absolutely crucial to understanding health-promoting patient behavior.

The case of the COVID-19 pandemic – compared to the last and rather similar polio pandemic – perhaps indicates that medicine has reached the limits of its capacity to provide relief: managing pandemics. Pandemics have ceased to be strictly a medical problem and are evolving into a social problem. While, with polio, the medications (vaccines) provided immediate relief ("there is salvation!") and yielded a solution to the problem because they were widely used, this same solution for solving today's problem is being challenged socially. The reluctance to embrace vaccines has resulted in an unimaginable increase in morbidity and mortality, and the risk that the pandemic will become a permanent feature of life. Psychologists from around the world are very intensively analyzing the various human behaviors that emerge, intensify, or disappear during a pandemic so that we can take an interdisciplinary approach to design better medical interventions aimed not only at fighting the current COVID-19 pandemic, but, we hope, at better preparing us for future pandemics that are surely on their way. It would be good for us to act as our parents and grandparents did during the polio outbreak by rapidly achieving protection.

This book is a contribution to these endeavors. The Polish National Agency for Academic Exchange grant (PPN/GIN/2020/1/00063/U/00001) that the first author of this book received allowed us to launch a research program addressing a fascinating property of the human mind: the falsification of reality to make it bearable, predictable, more optimistic in our eyes, as well as the positive and negative consequences of the actions of such an internal falsifier. The research that our international team has conducted has allowed us to uncover important empirical relationships and describe regularities that not only document how people function in the midst of a pandemic. It also, at least in part, may explain why, in such a specific situation of pervasive threat, some people follow medical advice and others, on the contrary, ignore it, leading to the persistence or progression of a pandemic when medicine provides effective tools for its complete elimination. Thus, we hope that this book will not only interest its readers, but also equip our medical colleagues with social science knowledge, so that the public response to the solutions they furnish will once again combat the pandemic as it did with polio.

This book consists of five parts. Since, as we noted above, pandemics have ceased to be a purely medical problem and have grown into a social problem as well, we have focused on the study of one of the psychological mechanisms that may have a great deal to do with whether a pandemic will end or last – the appearance of positive illusions during a pandemic. For this reason, the first chapter is a detailed presentation of two phenomena of such illusion creation and falsification of reality in such a way as to make it bearable: the better-than-average effect and unrealistic optimism.

In the second chapter, we present a number of empirical studies on the emergence of these illusions during the COVID-19 pandemic, and in the third chapter we analyze the relationship of these illusions to various health-promoting behaviors in the course of the coronavirus pandemic. The fourth chapter of the book is an attempt to present methods that can reduce the level of the aforementioned biases. (After all, while in everyday human life they in principle play a positive role, they can become dangerous in conditions of emergency). The fourth chapter then outlines methods to combat future pandemics because they are sure to come, and success in eradicating them may lie – as this book shows – in an interdisciplinary approach combining medicine and psychology. We devote the fifth and final chapter to reflecting on the non-medical consequences of COVID-19 (e.g., losses from school closures, psychological effects). Through this perspective, we want to show that failure to act appropriately on future widespread threats will increase the number of people affected by these consequences. Alternatively – thanks to this book, among other things – we will apply methods to combat the deadly illusions people may have about themselves.

Although only our names appear on the cover of this book, we can have no doubt that it was written due to the research conducted by our entire international team. We therefore take the liberty here of thanking for their collaboration Catherina Suitner and Bruno Salvador of the University of Padova, Italy; Oliver Genschow of Leuphana University Lüneburg, Germany; Ali Derakhshan of Golestan University, Iran; Aidana Rizulla of al-Farabi Kazakh National University, Kazakhstan; Daisy Winer of Brown University, USA; and a very large group of colleagues from Poland, especially Pawel Muniak, Kamil Izydorczak, and Tomasz Grzyb of SWPS University. After all, it must be borne in mind that science never develops in isolation. Both in designing our empirical research and in writing this book, we have benefited from the work of hundreds of others who have presented the results of their research in previously published books and articles. The reader will find their names in the References of this monograph. To them, too, we are obviously grateful. We extend our separate heartfelt appreciation to Matthew La Fontaine, thanks to whom this book reaches its readers written neatly in English. We also thank Michal Harciarek for neurobiological consultations.

We also express our gratitude to all the people who took the time to participate in our research. We would also like to thank the wonderful Springer team who helped us at various stages in our work on this book. We would like to mention here some of the names of those with whom we worked directly: Vijay Babu, Sharon Panulla, Amelie von Zumbusch, Dhivya Savariraj, Paige Ripperger, and Kala Palanisamy, but we know that a much larger group of people employed by the publisher were involved in the creation of this volume. Institutionally, we thank the Polish National Agency for Academic Exchange not only for funding our work, whose results we may present here, but especially for the fact that the electronic edition of this manuscript is fully free for you, the readers of these words. We have also received tremendous support from our SWPS University. The period covered by our research included a time when our workplace was closed and all collaboration moved online. Without the tools provided to us, it would have been impossible to conduct our work.

While thanking once again all the people and institutions mentioned above, at the same time we want to emphasize that any errors, ambiguities, or understatements you may find in this book are our sole responsibility. We write this with the dangers of the positive illusions that we analyze in this monograph in mind. In accordance with them, we should believe that it is others, not us, who make mistakes. So we humbly admit that the opposite is true – it is we who are responsible for any failings.

Warsaw, Poland — Wojciech Kulesza
Wroclaw, Poland — Dariusz Doliński

Endorsements

"The authors, two well-respected social psychologists from Poland, have written a book explaining how common, everyday biases in how we see ourselves and the world can have important negative consequences for how we react to and cope with emergencies and catastrophes. Their primary thesis, which they support with numerous citations from their own and others' work, is that people tend to "ignore the downside" and "focus on the upside" when they evaluate potential risks. Highly recommended for those who are curious about how the cognitive biases of individuals can affect how society deals with large-scale challenges." – **John Nezlek,** College of William & Mary, USA, SWPS University, Poland

"In this timely and important book, Kulesza and Dolinski document the many crises that humanity faces today and show how these challenges are magnified by the cognitive biases inherent in human nature. They argue that awareness of these biases does not doom us to succumb to dysfunctional behavior, but rather provides the knowledge we need to meet the challenges of living in a precarious world." – **Robin R. Vallacher**, Florida Atlantic University, USA

"Kudos to Drs. Kulesza and Dolinski! This book is a timely and entertainingly examination of the comparative biases that pervade our judgements about our risk for COVID and other unwanted outcomes and what we can do to reduce the biases." – **James A. Shepperd**, University of Florida, USA

Contents

About the Authors

Wojciech Kulesza is Associate Professor, Chair of Social Psychology Department, SWPS University. Researches, publishes, and teaches across three main disciplines: (1) mimicry/the chameleon effect, (2) social biases in decision making, and (3) psychology of love. Currently involved in interdisciplinary research on the anti-vaccination movement.

Dariusz Doliński is Professor and Chair, Head of Social Psychology Department in SWPS University, Department of Psychology in Wroclaw, past President of Polish Association of Social Psychology, and past Editor-in-Chief of *Polish Psychological Bulletin*. Researcher working in the area of social influence. Author of 24 books and more than 250 articles. Currently involved in interdisciplinary research concerning the anti-vaccination movement.

Chapter 1
The Unbearable Darkness of Being and a Toolkit for How We Forge It: Comparative Biases

1.1 Realism, Illusions, or Even Delusions?

Conceiving of mental health and good adjustment in terms of individuals' accurate perception of the world around them and of themselves seems virtually self-evident. In other words, psychiatry's interest includes analyzing whether we perceive ourselves and the outside world as they are or whether we distort, or falsify, both of these images. Psychiatry identifies loss of contact with reality, delusions, and delusional beliefs of patients that they are someone other than they really are as axial symptoms of mental illness (e.g., Meisner et al., 2021; Zandersen & Parnas, 2019). Psychology as well, until the late 1960s, was convinced that mental health and good adjustment were closely related to realism: accuracy in assessing one's own mental qualities and potential for success in various areas of life or a person's mature, realistic attribution of responsibility for both positive and negative events that befall them. Such a belief was characteristic of both those strands of psychology that were humanistic (e.g., Horney; 1937; Maslow, 1954) and strictly cognitive (e.g., Festinger, 1954; Trope, 1975). This is different; it was thought, in the case of people whose mental health is disturbed, because then the "images" (of themselves, the world) are falsified. And this does not apply only to obvious clinical cases of psychosis but to much more subtle illusions, which are typical for almost all people (and therefore also for us, the authors of this book). For example, the theory of cognitive dissonance (Festinger, 1954) reveals that if, along with a paltry salary, we have worked on something for a very long time or if we have been in a relationship with another person for years with no apparent achievements coming from our relationship, when asked about the meaningfulness of our endeavors, we will respond in a manner that allows us to maintain a good opinion of ourselves. Instead of saying that we worked for years for a pittance on something terribly boring, we will say that it is not boring at all. Instead of admitting that we are stuck in a bad relationship, we will say that it has its pluses. And all this is only because we retroactively justify to ourselves that "since I have invested so much, it must have meaning."

W. Kulesza, D. Doliński, *Social Biases During Covid 19*, SpringerBriefs in Psychology, https://doi.org/10.1007/978-3-031-34706-1_1

It is a common belief that depressed people look at the world through gloomy lenses, thus overestimating the likelihood of negative events and underestimating the chances that desirable states of affairs will occur. However, is this really the case? In 1979, a very interesting article by Lauren Alloy and Lyn Abramson was published, whose subtitle labels depressed people "sadder but wiser." The research of these authors showed that depressed people show more realism in assessing themselves and their ability to influence the course of events than nondepressed people. In other words, it is rather well-adjusted people who seem to have very rose-colored glasses on, rather than depressed people wearing glasses that obscure reality. This result, although shocking from a certain perspective, was perfectly in line with the notion, gradually emerging in scientific psychology at the time, that mental health and good adjustment are not at all served by an accurate and fully realistic view of oneself and the world around us.

In the realm of social psychology, Anthony Greenwald (1980) introduced the term "totalitarian ego" into the literature, showing in a series of studies that mentally healthy people make (usually unconscious) distortions of their own memory. Our ego resembles the regime functionary from George Orwell's famous book "1984" (1949/2021). This functionary constantly and consistently changes the content of newspaper articles in the library from years ago so that it is in conformity with the (current) party line (much like a censor, which, as an aside, we experienced for ourselves, since until 1989 we lived in a communist country where censors changed not only the content of news but even ordinary songs). We behave similarly – we remember things so that they are consistent with our positive self-perception (e.g., we don't remember that we showed ignorance in a conversation with another person, lied, or hurt other people) and so that they do not shatter our conviction of our own competence or morality ("I'm a good, truthful person"). Significantly, from the perspective discussed here, Greenwald shows that such "totalitarian" inclinations of our ego are functional: they serve not only our well-being but also provide a coherent and stable view of ourselves, helping us to make appropriate life decisions and stimulating our achievements.

Ellen Langer (1975) showed, in turn, the prevalence of the human tendency to manifest the illusion of control. People seem to believe that they have influence over purely random events. When they play dice and there is a lot of money on the table, they shake the dice in the cup longer and then more carefully toss them on the table. When they take part in a traditional lottery, they are unlikely to reach for the ticket lying on the very top. They prefer to put their hand inside the box, stir the tickets with their hand, and pull one out from underneath. When they have to bet on something and the verdict will be whether a tossed coin will fall "heads or tails," they prefer to bet before the coin is tossed rather than when it is already lying on the table and they only need guess what you see on it. Apparently, if the coin has not yet been tossed, we can concentrate and somehow influence with our stream of thought or energy the probability of heads showing. If the coin is already in place, we can only guess.

At the same time, studies have begun appearing in increasing numbers in the psychological literature showing that people are not necessarily oriented toward seeking believable diagnoses of themselves. On the contrary, they are extremely often biased to seek rather such information that can provide them with a rationale for thinking positively about themselves, and they block, distort, or avoid such information that could disrupt this positive thinking (e.g., Korman, 1976; Suls, 1977; Goethals, 1986). Thus, one can clearly see how many fields we deceive ourselves in so as to simplify life. Like the aforementioned totalitarian censor from "1984," we falsify reality because it is easier and more beautiful for us to live that way.

These and other numerous manifestations of inadequate attitudes of mentally healthy people toward themselves and the external world formed the basis of Shelley Taylor and Jonathon Brown's (1988) groundbreaking psychology article with the highly suggestive and unambiguous title of "Illusions and Well-Being. A Social Psychological Perspective on Mental Health." Reviewing a very large number of empirical studies, these authors conclude that the so-called "normal," i.e., well-functioning and effective, people manifest three types of falsifications, positive illusions about themselves. So, first of all, they are characterized by an inadequate, inflated concept of self-worth (and thus, compared to the opinions of others who know them, they rate their intelligence or social competencies higher). One phenomenon of this type, better than average, is analyzed more extensively in this monograph. Second, such people are characterized by the aforementioned illusion of control. They see their influence on desirable, positive events even though realistically they do not have this influence or they estimate this influence to be higher than it actually is. Third, they are characterized by the so-called unrealistic optimism, which is discussed at length in the context of COVID-19 in subsequent chapters. Then, when, for example, university students estimate the likelihood of desirable events in their lives (such as having a happy family in the future or pursuing a career that is both rewarding to them and well-paid), they estimate that they are more likely to do so than most of their peers. However, when they think about potential negative events (such as having a heart attack before turning 40, contracting AIDS, or sliding into alcoholism), they believe it is less likely to happen to them than to the average student in their class. Summing up this important work, Taylor and Brown (1988) conclude that the falsified image is beneficial: it carries clear benefits for the falsifier – the totalitarian censor.

Later studies have enriched the picture now familiar to readers of the relationship between positive illusions and well-being (e.g., Boyd-Wilson et al., 2004; Collard et al., 2016) with results showing that in many situations this relationship may be more complex than psychologists initially thought. In their article, Dufner et al. (2019) present the results of a meta-analytic review involving as many as 299 studies with a total of 129,916 participants. They show that the tendency to maintain unrealistically positive self-views is positively related to personal adjustment (life satisfaction, positive affect, infrequent experiencing of negative affect and depressive states), but the associations of positive illusions with interpersonal adjustment (informant reports of domain-general social valuation, agency and communion) were found to be weak. Brooking and Serratelli (2006), on the other hand, show data indicating that positive illusions about the self and the world correlate positively with subjective well-being, but their relationship with measures of personal growth is negative. In other words, in addition to gains, losses from a falsified image of self and the world were also indicated. A review of the literature by Young (2014) also came to similar conclusions. The not entirely consistent and not entirely conclusive findings on the relationship between positive illusions and subject functioning may be due to two facts, among others.

First, Roy Baumeister (1989) pointed out that positive illusions can optimize human functioning only when their magnitude is not too great. However, they become self-destructive when they increase in intensity. Thus, while a moderately unrealistic perception of one's own abilities, skills, and character traits ("I think I'm a bit smarter than others") is characteristic of mentally healthy people, an overly exaggeratedly favorable perception of oneself ("I'm brilliant and can easily handle any situation") is usually associated with an individual experiencing mental issues. Baumeister thus speaks of the optimal margin of illusion. If this threshold is exceeded in the direction of reinforcing falsification, the term "illusion" should no longer be used (e.g., "rose-colored glasses" would be an inappropriate term here). Much more apt in this situation would be the term "delusion" – a completely falsified image of oneself and/or the world.

Empirical evidence for the validity of this approach was provided by Asendorpf and Ostendoerf (1998). They showed unequivocally that exaggerated favorable self-perceptions are usually associated with an individual's experience of psychological problems. The negative consequences of exaggerated positive illusions in the context of psychotherapy are discussed, in turn, by Kinney (2000), suggesting that they set in motion various irrational mental processes that are an obstacle to patients' mature and healthy perception of their problems. Concurrent with this approach are the results of clinical studies suggesting that in situations involving various negative events in a person's life, overly positive self-perception is a significant factor in the development of depression (Young-Hoon & Chi-Yue, 2011). Nonclinical studies show, in turn, that greatly heightened positive illusions can be an obstacle to students' achievement of good grades (Ochse, 2012).

Second, Peter Gollwitzer (1996) reasonably argues that if positive illusions occur in the so-called implemental phase, i.e., accompanying the execution of the action itself, they promote the effective implementation of resolutions, immunize against difficulties, and motivate to overcome them. Consequently, they increase the individual's effectiveness. However, if such illusions occur in the deliberative phase, that is, when deciding to take action or choosing the degree of difficulty of the action, they can be destructive, because the actor chooses tasks that are too difficult, overestimating their level of competence and/or nourishing an unreasonable hope that over time the situation will arrange itself so favorably that they will be able to cope with the task. These assumptions, too, have been confirmed in empirical studies (e.g., Armor & Taylor, 2003; O'Creery et al., 2010). Interestingly, the vast majority of well-functioning, mentally healthy people suspend (or at least limit) the experience of positive illusions in the deliberative phase and only reveal them in the implemental phase (e.g., Gollwitzer, 2003; Gollwitzer & Kinney, 1989; Puca, 2001). Thus, it can be said that a person behaves rationally when it is beneficial and becomes somewhat irrational only when the very activation of positive illusions can help them. (Or, looking at the same problem from a different perspective, a typical person lives by illusions when it is beneficial but suspends them when following them becomes dangerous.) This perspective will accompany us in the following chapters of this book where we will demonstrate how many of the illusions that we ourselves actively build can help us and, at the same time, how they can harm us.

1.2 Social Comparison and Egotism

The aforementioned esteemed social psychologist Leon Festinger formulated the social comparison theory, the axial premise of which is the proposition that people strive to accurately assess their skills, possibilities, and also want to be convinced of the accuracy of the opinions they express (Festinger, 1954). Festinger even refers to this motivation with the term "drive" (p. 117), usually reserved for aspirations of a biological nature, such as the need to satisfy hunger and thirst or to gratify sexual needs. He is, of course, far from suggesting that the drive to know oneself is a phenomenon of a biological, impulsive nature; rather, by using the term "drive" metaphorically, he wants to emphasize both the universality and the intensity of this need. According to Festinger, people primarily try to obtain information about themselves from objective sources. To check the accuracy of one's own views about the size of the population in India or the height of Mount K2, it is easiest to turn to relevant, reliable printed sources or, in today's times, the Internet. Knowledge of one's skills and abilities (e.g., IQ test score) can be obtained by performing certain diagnostic tasks (e.g., completing a reliable intelligence test). This also applies to other capabilities. If a 40-year-old woman wants to find out if she can swim a kilometer, she goes to the pool and gives it a try. Also, knowledge about the state of one's own physical condition (e.g., whether we have a fever) can be obtained through unambiguous tests (using a thermometer). On the other hand, if we want to know what our cholesterol level is, we submit a blood sample to a laboratory and find out from the doctor either that everything is normal or that we should start treatment because we are not healthy.

However, in many other cases, it is not possible to evaluate oneself so directly. If the aforementioned woman would like to find out not only whether she can swim a kilometer (this she has already verified for herself and knows she can) but also whether she can do it quickly, there is little to be gained from the fact that she managed to do it in, say, 39 min. To answer the question "how fast do I swim?," she must make interpersonal comparisons. Only by relating this result to, for example, such data as the unofficial women's world record (since no competitions are officially held at this distance) or the performance exhibited by her mother, daughter, or coworkers at the moment can she identify the basis of any assessment of herself. Thus, if information about oneself is not directly available from nonpersonal sources, one is fated to obtain it by comparing one's own opinions, capabilities, skills and abilities with those of other people. Indeed, adequate knowledge of oneself is that which Festinger assumed humans earnestly strive for, and that is why he called this need "drive."

In Festinger's concept, the question of who the subject compares himself with is not without relevance. Returning to our example, the diagnostic value of comparisons with a world record holder, a 70-year-old mother, and work colleagues is markedly different. According to Festinger, given a variety of people to potentially choose from in the process of social comparison, individuals choose those who are similar to themselves and/or are in a similar situation. For a 40-year-old woman, comparing herself with both her mother, who last swam at a Girl Scout camp 65 years ago, and with a world record holder is hardly diagnostic. However, the most information she can get about her swimming skills (or physical form more broadly) is by comparing herself with other 40-year-old females (preferably ones who, like her, are working professionally, have suffered a heart attack, and also have raised three children).

However, people are not always motivated to compare themselves with others who are similar. When it comes to assessing one's own abilities and skills, we can also acquire useful information by comparing ourselves with people who are better than us. This is because by doing so, we gain knowledge of how much we are missing to achieve a certain desired state. Someone learning a foreign language can compare themself with a colleague proficient in that language, observing over successive months and years that they consistently deviate less and less (but still) from them in performance.

That said, research on social comparison processes, inspired by Festinger's (1954) ideas, has shown that people's preferences for choosing others to benchmark themselves against are much more complex than the author of social comparison theory believed and that the desire to obtain diagnostic information about oneself is not the only motivation driving people to compare themselves with others.

Bib Latané (1966), while not refuting the basic thesis of Festinger's concept, which is that, in the absence of objective criteria, people are inclined to derive evaluative knowledge about themselves from comparisons they make between themselves and others, pointed out at the same time that the purpose behind this is not necessarily to obtain reliable and diagnostic information. He suggested that people often seek information that confirms their judgments about themselves, rather than information that might significantly undermine that knowledge. This is because people are reluctant to change their views not only about the physical and social world around them but also about themselves. Both classics (e.g., Swann, 1983, 1987; Swann & Read, 1981) and new, more contemporary empirical studies (e.g., Hart et al., 2009; Gregg et al., 2017) have shown that this is indeed the case in many situations.

Based on the hypotheses of Latane, who illustrated the biased nature of comparisons, other researchers assumed that the core motivation in the process of social comparison is also biased, but primarily defensive and therefore egotistical (e.g., Jellison & Davis, 1973; Gruder, 1971; Goethals, 1986). This is associated with the fact that people primarily seek such information that can raise and enhance their self-esteem (self-enhancement). This is particularly common in situations where someone making comparisons is experiencing stress or suffering negative emotions or their self-esteem is threatened for various reasons (e.g., Hahmiller, 1966; Wills, 1981, 1987). The need for this individual to compare themself with others who are inferior – thus falsifying the objective image – grows. This is because we cannot come off badly by comparing ourselves with objectively weaker, inferior people. The aforementioned woman will compare herself with people in a swimming school for kindergarteners, while someone else will compare their IQ score with people who have little knowledge of the language in which the diagnostic test is conducted. In doing so, such comparisons can be passive (selecting people who are actually less competent or talented than the subject for comparison) or active (attributing negative qualities to other people that they do not actually have). Consequently, this shows that the aforementioned censor employs a number of ploys that go beyond "1984": not only does he retroactively alter the records of facts but also the perception of human qualities. Numerous pieces of empirical evidence indicate that such comparisons with inferior others improve people's well-being (e.g., Crocker & Gallo, 1985), as well as increase their self-confidence (e.g., Lemyre & Smith, 1985). This means that such falsifications are beneficial to us in some manner.

Thus, we see that comparisons with other people may not only serve the purpose of accurately recognizing one's competence and capabilities, as Festinger assumed. On the contrary, in many cases, people may be concerned primarily with avoiding diagnostic information about themselves when comparisons may be unflattering, while at the same time acquiring such information that allows them to assess their own competencies, abilities, and potential capabilities very positively. Psychology has accumulated both ample evidence of the prevalence of such motivations and the occurrence of a wide variety of sometimes highly sophisticated behaviors that allow people to prevent information from reaching them that could threaten their self-esteem, while being open to any information that reinforces and boosts self-confidence (e.g., Leary, 2007; Grosser et al., 2021; Jelic, 2022).

Summarizing this section and indicating what we will later discuss, let us note that comparing oneself with others does not necessarily mean confronting one's own qualities, competencies, or abilities with those of some other, specific person (a swimmer compares herself with people in a swimming school). Indeed, in certain situations, people may rather compare themselves with an abstracted "average person" or estimate what percentage of people in a certain population they are better or worse than in certain respects.

We will describe two such phenomena – the better-than-average effect (BTAE) and unrealistic optimism (UO) – more extensively below, since people's manifestation of them, as well as the consequences of this state for their functioning, became the subject of our empirical inquiries at a time when the world was affected by the coronavirus pandemic. We will also present the effects of such comparisons (especially regarding the manifestation of health-seeking behavior) in the context of the COVID-19 pandemic. We will see whether these social illusions benefit or harm the faker.

1.3 Better-than-Average Effect

Let's start with a reminder that one of the three basic positive illusions that Taylor and Brown (1988) wrote about in their now classic article was inadequate, inflated confidence in one's own worth. Well-functioning people judge their own competence and other desirable qualities better than they should from an objective point of view. The better-than-average effect is one manifestation of just such an overly positive self-perception. Psychological research on this effect involves asking participants to rate the strength of some trait, ability, or skill they possess by comparing themselves with other people.

In one classic study of the better-than-average effect (Alicke et al., 1995), college students were asked to rate the extent to which they possessed 20 positive personality or character traits (such as intelligent, honorable, reliable, or responsible) and 20 negative traits (such as deceptive, humorless, snobbish, or liar) compared to the average college student of their sex. They used a 9-point scale to do this each time: from 0 and the phrase "much less than average college student" on the left end to 8 and the phrase "much more than average college student." The middle value was 4, "about the same as the average college student."

Logically, it could follow that some students should consider themselves "better" than others, some as equal, and some as "worse." It turned out that the majority of those surveyed felt that positive designations better suited them than the average student, while negative designations better suited the average student than them. What a strange result! After all, it's impossible for everyone to be better than the average person! The individual values presented in this table represent the degree to which the average estimates for "self" deviate from the middle value of 4. Obviously, positive numbers mean that the respondents believe that the trait describes them better than it does the average student (comparisons that result in portraying themselves in a positive light), and negative numbers mean that it fits the average student to a greater extent than it does them.

In doing so, let us note that among people who describe themselves as better (in certain respects) than the average person, there may be both those who are actually better, those who are average, and those who, realistically speaking, are worse. Thus, in the case of people belonging to the former group, it is difficult to treat such estimates as an illusion or to refer to them as bias. Note, however, that only half of the population surveyed can be better than the average person. This is because participants are comparing themselves to an average person, not to an average value. The distribution of a particular value may be such that more than 50% of the population can be better than average. For example, 62% of a country's population may earn above the average salary in that country. This will be the case if a sizable portion of that country's population lives in poverty. Also, 58% of the population may eat more meat than the average per capita consumption of meat. This will be the case if a large group of people don't eat meat at all or eat meat very rarely and in small amounts. But the logic of the better-than-average effect is different. The individual does not compare to the average value, but to the average person.

With reference to the study mentioned above (Alicke et al., 1995), at most, every second college student can be better than the average college student. Thus, if more than 50% consider themselves better, then some of them simply cannot be correct. The better-than-average effect thus refers to an illusion we observe at group level, stating that it is shared by a portion of the population. At the same time, this part increases in size together with the extent to which the group of people who consider themselves better than the average person exceeds the magic barrier of 50%. At the same time, it should be emphasized that even if literally all respondents claimed to be better than the average person (e.g., they all thought they were more intelligent than the average person), we could only speak of bias with regard to half of them. (After all, half may indeed be more intelligent than this average as much as half could be less intelligent.) Be that as it may, the research presented above is excellent evidence of the workings of the falsifier-censor: I believe that I am better than others! Someone – and no small part of those participating – must be falsely positive in their self-assessment!

A similar regularity revealing the tendency of most people to see themselves as better than average was also noted by Jonathon Brown (1986), but using a slightly different method of measurement. The participants first estimated to what extent they themselves had various positive and negative qualities and then to what extent the average person had these qualities. This time, therefore, the better-than-average effect can be ascertained from the difference in estimates of the self and the average other. However, this method of measurement, different from that used by Alicke et al., did not affect the recorded result, which illustrates how universal and robust the described process is. It turned out that people as active censors not only falsify the past to match the present but also falsify the present to maintain a positive self-image. To achieve this, they ascribe positive traits to themselves to a greater extent than to the "average other," and when it comes to negative traits, they see less of them in themselves than in the average person.

Still another method employed in psychological research to measure the better-than-average effect was to have participants select one of two responses: "below average" or "above average," when answering the question to what extent they possessed certain (negative and positive) traits. Perhaps the most spectacular (at least in terms of results) study conducted in this paradigm revealed that 94% of teachers considered themselves to be better educators than the average teacher (Cross, 1977). This means that hardly any of them were worse than average! Let us note here in passing that the disadvantage of this distinct paradigm, compared to those previously described, is the impossibility of defining oneself as entirely similar to the average person – one can only be better or worse than them, which of course is inconsistent with what at least some people may actually think of themselves. Of course, this inconvenience can be easily avoided by introducing a third option for participants to choose from: "about the same as an average person."

Some researchers have followed a more precise approach to determining the strength of the better-than-average effect. Here, the participant is asked to give the percentage of people from an own group (e.g., the percentage of students of their sex at the college they attend) compared to which they possess a given (positive or negative) trait to a greater degree. If we imagine a scale from 0% (no one) to 100% (everyone), its center would be a value of 50% (half of the people in that group). Thus, an average score significantly above 50% for desirable traits, or significantly below 50% for undesirable traits, will indicate the presence of a better-than-average effect in the population under study because such a self-reporting distortion (attributing positive traits to oneself while attributing negative ones to others) casts the person in an extremely positive light.

The classic study conducted in such a paradigm is one in which students with drivers' licenses from both the United States (University of Oregon) and Sweden (University of Stockholm) quantified their competence as automobile drivers (Svenson, 1981). The study was a collective one, and the participants were tasked with estimating the proportion (in percent) of those in the room that the given participant drives more safely than and of those who are more skillful drivers. As we will see in Table 1.1, the majority of people surveyed from both countries believed that they drive more safely than most other students and have better driving skills, which of course is simply objectively impossible.

The better-than-average effect with regard to being a driver can be vividly illustrated by the example of driving on the highway. From time to time, we overtake some vehicles, and from time to time, some vehicles overtake us. What do we think of other drivers? Those we overtake are most likely driving slowly because they lack skills and therefore drive overcautiously. They are simply poor drivers. Those who overtake us, on the other hand, are lunatics, "organ donors" who think that they alone can drive well, while they in fact compensate for their lack of skill with needless bravado. So, in our own eyes, we are better highway drivers than both those who drive slower than us and faster than us.

However, the means of identifying the better-than-average effect – by indicating the percentage of people whom one is better than – has one serious drawback: when we are not dealing with a normal distribution, ambiguity enters into the picture. If we assume, for example, that one-third of participants believe that they are better in some respect than as many as 90% of people and most of the remaining participants estimate that they are better than, say, 45%, serious difficulties with interpretation

Table 1.1 Distribution of percent of estimates over degree of safe and skillful driving in relation to other drivers

	Estimated position in sample (percentiles)									
	0–10	11–20	21–30	31–40	41–50	51–60	61–70	71–80	81–90	91–100
Safety										
US sample	2.5	0.0	5.0	0.0	5.0	2.5	2.5	22.5	37.5	22.5
Swedish sample	0.0	5.7	0.0	14.3	2.9	11.4	14.3	28.6	17.1	5.7
Skill										
US sample	0.0	2.4	2.4	2.4	0.0	12.2	22.0	12.2	26.8	19.5
Swedish sample	2.2	6.7	2.2	4.4	15.5	17.7	11.1	24.4	13.3	2.2

Higher percentiles represent less risky and more skilful driving
Source: *Acta Psychologica, 47*, p. 145
Copyright: Elsevier

arise. After all, depending on the perspective taken, in such a situation, it is possible to conclude that the better-than-average effect is present (the average estimate exceeds being better than 50% of people) or that it is not present. (In our opinion, the latter conclusion would be correct, since only a clear minority of people believe that they are significantly better than the vast majority of people in a certain respect, while the majority believe that they are among the worse half.) Let us add for the sake of clarity that we are not aware of any case in which the doubts we have presented actually appeared in psychological research on the effect we describe here. In other words, the body of literature on this subject does not allow us to cast doubt on the universality of the belief in one's own "superiority."

The use by researchers of the four distinct approaches detailed above to measuring the better-than-average effect does sometimes complicate the comparison of results recorded in particular empirical studies, but, on the other hand, it increases our confidence that we are dealing with a real, robust, and prevalent psychological phenomenon. This does not mean, of course, that people consider themselves better than others (or better than the average person) in terms of all possible qualities and competencies. This is described by the phenomenon sometimes termed the "Muhammad Ali effect."

Muhammad Ali is considered by many boxing fans to be the greatest fighter of all time. One anecdote involving Ali says that when he was questioned by a journalist about his intelligence, he replied that he never considered himself intelligent nor does he think he is smarter than other athletes or other boxers. At the same time, he explained that he is simply much faster than others, which ensures his success in the ring. As he put it, "I'm so fast that last night I turned off the light switch in my hotel room and was in bed before the room was dark."

As Paul Van Lange (1991) has shown, most people do not claim to be superior to others in all positive respects. The Muhammad Ali effect assumes that belief in one's own superiority is limited to selected characteristics. In most cases, it is more important for people to believe that they are more moral than most others than to hold the belief that they are more competent than others (Van Lange & Sedikides, 1998). In the case of competence, people only believe they are better than the average person in their chosen areas (e.g., they think, "I am a better driver than most people, but I certainly don't dance better than the average person of my sex").

However, since individual people may see this self-betterness in relation to different traits and competencies, the overall picture emerging from empirical research indicates that the better-than-average effect is largely universal. In other words, the sphere of comparison is as extensive as the number of traits or other personal characteristics being compared. It should thus come as no surprise that people's belief that they are better than others in a wide range of mental traits, skills, and competencies has been evidenced in a multitude of studies (see Chambers & Windschitl, 2004; Zell et al., 2020, for review), further indicating the robustness of this effect. In yet other studies, it has been shown that, in addition to the aforementioned competencies or positive psychological traits, people also consider themselves better than others with regard to the frequency and intensity of various behaviors. Thus, for example, Leviston and Uren (2020) showed that most of the people they surveyed consider themselves more involved in environmentally friendly activities than others. In turn, a number of other studies indicate that people believe they are more likely to be involved in various charitable endeavors than most other people (e.g., Brown, 2012; Epley & Dunning, 2000). Still other studies reveal that people believe they eat much healthier than others (Scherer et al., 2016) and even that they eat for "better" reasons than others. This is because people declare that they themselves eat mainly because they are simply hungry and the food they choose is tasty and healthy. Others, they say, eat for different and not necessarily praiseworthy reasons: they want to make a desirable impression on others, conform to social norms, or make themselves feel better through food (Sproesser et al., 2017).

What is particularly interesting is that comparisons can concern traits that are unusually strongly related to being, the morality that makes us human. For example, Dolinski and Grzyb (2020) conducted an extensive research program on obedience that drew on the famous experiments of Stanley Milgram (1963, 1965, 1974). In these studies, individuals were invited into a laboratory, and it was explained to them that they would be participating in an experiment on the effect of punishment on learning performance. Their task was to step into the role of a teacher and electrocute a "student" (in fact a confederate of the experimenter, who only suggestively feigned suffering). The student was to be punished for each successive mistake with an increasingly powerful jolt. A special apparatus was used to administer punishment – an electric current generator, equipped with 30 switches, the first of which was marked with the symbol 15 V, and each subsequent one was correspondingly marked 15 V higher. Thus, the second switch was marked with 30 V and the third with 45 V, and the last was marked with 450 V. The experiment ended when the participants categorically refused further cooperation or when they successively pressed all 30 switches.

Dolinski and Grzyb studied various personality and situational determinants of participants' behavior in such a situation (for ethical reasons, they stopped the study as soon as the participant pressed the tenth switch, labeled 150 V), but they also conducted one study in which they explored people's beliefs about the behavior of people who are instructed by a psychologist to electrocute another person in the lab (Grzyb & Dolinski, 2017). The participants were presented with Milgram's experiment in detail, and they were asked to judge both how they themselves would behave in the experiment and how other participants would act. In doing so, these other participants were referred to variously as an "average person" (in general), as well as an "average person of the same nationality" (the research was conducted in Poland), alongside questions about "average people" of several other nationalities. Each time, the participants were asked to indicate the last switch that a participant in the Milgram experiment would press. As we will see in Table 1.2, participants were convinced that they themselves would terminate their participation in the experiment much sooner than others. In other words, they declared that they were more moral people, less likely to visit evil on an innocent stranger. Importantly, these declarations are easily juxtaposed with the participants' actual behavior (in Milgram's original study and many subsequent replications), which showed that more or less two-thirds of them acted unethically by applying all possible punishments to the "student."

Table 1.2 The voltage of the last switch that the participants indicated in particular responses (myself, average person, average Pole, etc.)

Nation	Mean	Standard error	95% Confidence interval	
			Lower bound	Upper bound
Average person	181.782	6.239	169.528	194.035
I (myself)	102.223	5.449	91.521	112.925
Pole	169.535	5.422	158.885	180.186
German	190.442	6.056	178.546	202.338
Russian	240.875	6.193	228.710	253.040
Englishman	133.737	4.755	124.398	143.076
Frenchman	134.189	4.980	124.408	143.970

Source: *Frontiers in Psychology*, fpsyh.2017.01632 Tab. 1

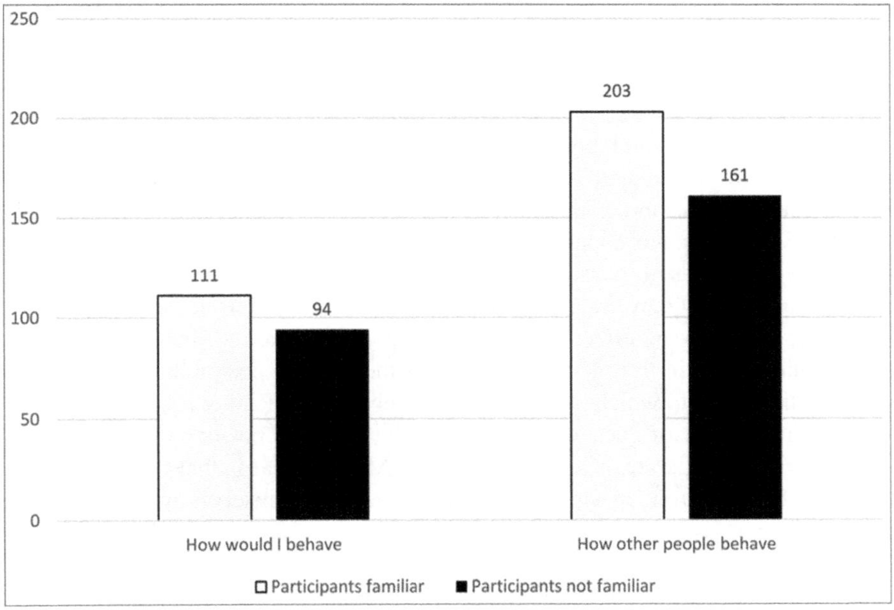

Fig. 1.1 Means in questions "how would I behave" and "how other people behave" in group familiar and not familiar with Milgram experiment
Source: *Frontiers in Psychology* fpsyh.2017.01632, Figure 1

The majority of participants in the study by Grzyb and Dolinsky had only just learned about the Milgram experiment scenario, but as there were also some with prior knowledge of Milgram's research, they should have been more rational, less biased. It turned out that prior knowledge of this shocking experiment modified beliefs about how other people would behave but did not affect beliefs about one's own behavior (the differences in the two groups were not statistically significant) nor did it reduce the better-than-average effect (see Fig. 1.1). Thus, it can be said that knowledge of the Milgram experiment scenario and its results impacted judgments about other people but did not make a difference in beliefs about oneself, thus demonstrating how strong the better-than-average effect is. Despite knowledge of the experiment's results, we still persist in portraying ourselves in a more positive light.

As we approach the conclusion of this section, let us take a look at the issue from a broader perspective. As with all other psychological phenomena, in addition to "the way it is" (this we already know), it is necessary to ask "why is it so?" In other words, we inquire as to the psychological mechanism underlying the better-than-average effect: why do we exhibit the tendency to falsify our perception of the world and ourselves in it? The empirical material accumulated so far gives us cause to assume that the motivation to protect and boost one's self-esteem lies at its core. This is because, first of all, it has been shown that the aforementioned effect is stronger when the characteristics being compared are important (vs. less important) to the participant (Brown, 2012; Ziano et al., 2020), as well as when they are important (vs. less important) from the perspective of the culture in which the research is conducted (Sedikides et al., 2003; Lee, 2012). In addition, the effect analyzed here is stronger when people compare themselves to others on abstract dimensions (Dunning et al., 1989) and those for which it is difficult to develop objective criteria for verifying the accuracy of estimates (Van Lange & Sedikides, 1998). Also worth mentioning here are studies in which belief in one's own "superiority" rose immediately after participants experienced threats to their self-esteem (Brown, 2012).

However, on a case-by-case basis, cognitive mechanisms can reinforce or weaken people's beliefs that they are better than others. It has been shown, for example, that the better-than-average effect weakens when people are asked first to estimate to what extent a certain trait is characteristic of the average person and only then to estimate the extent to which it applies to themselves (e.g., Pahl & Eiser, 2007). This change in the order of questions means that the typically positive opinion held of oneself ceases to operate as a reference point. Also peculiar is that the better-than-average effect is stronger when participants compare themselves with an abstract "average other" as opposed to a specific person (e.g., a family member or friend). This can be explained by the fact that information about self is usually cognitively accessible to the individual: we know more about our own actions or qualities than about the actions or qualities of others, even those closest to us. Thus, we may feel superior to the "average other" because we know nothing about this abstract figure, while we know quite a bit about ourselves. However, if we are asked to compare ourself to a particular friend or spouse, the difference in the availability of information about ourself and about this other person is much smaller precisely because we know much more about them – if only because of a familiarity bred over years spent together – than about, for example, neighbors we rarely see (Kruger, 1999).

To summarize here the research on the phenomenon described in this section, we would like to present the conclusions of a meta-analysis of studies on the better-than-average effect (Zell et al., 2020). The main results presented by the authors of these studies can be summarized as follows:

1. Better than average is highly robust across studies, with overall effect size that vary from large to very large. It should be added here that the effect size is clearly larger than that usually recorded in psychological studies, which shows that this effect is extremely strong.
2. The better-than-average effect is weaker under conditions in which participants are addressing positive attributes or competencies than when they compare themselves with others concerning negative attributes.
3. The better-than-average effect is stronger among young people than older ones.
4. Participants' sex and race did not influence the magnitude of the reported better-than-average effect.

1.4 Unrealistic Optimism

An earlier chapter explored how we make false comparisons as regards our own traits. We attribute desirable qualities to ourselves and negative qualities to others. As we are about to see, this is not the only way in which the censor rewrites reality. This time, the falsification concerns not fixed qualities but rather events in everyday life that can affect us all. Thus, we should all reasonably expect that, whether good or bad, they will happen to both us and others with the same probability.

Every individual's life is inevitably at risk of a traffic mishap, natural disaster, the loss of one's home, or an (incurable) illness. Desirable things can (and sometimes do) also happen to each of us: an interesting job, a successful marriage, healthy and talented children, or a fascinating vacation in an exotic country. Armed with knowledge of the better-than-average effect, you are likely already predicting (correctly) that people attribute probabilities (positive vs. negative) of events to ourselves and others irrationally and unequally. And you are correct! However, before we explore this phenomenon, we begin with an introduction to optimism.

Numerous psychological studies that are now considered classics of the literature have demonstrated that we believe desirable events are more likely to happen than they actually are, while undesirable events seem less likely to us than objective circumstances would indicate (Marx, 1951; Irwin, 1953). There is also a fairly common tendency to see the present as better than the past and the future as better than the present (Matlin & Stang, 1978). Although the sources of this optimistic view of one's future remain in dispute, the prevalence of such an attitude toward the possible course of events is undisputed. Most people are characterized by an optimistic attitude toward reality, and this attitude is activated in most situations (Seligman, 1998).

We write in this book about positive illusions. As you might imagine, our focus here is on precisely such optimism characterized by falsification and illusion, which is not an objectively sensible perception of the world. The very term "unrealistic optimism" clearly indicates reference to a positive expectation of future events that, at least partially, is divorced from reality. Psychology understands unrealistic optimism in two ways. First, we define positive estimates as unrealistic if we confront them with an objective criterion, allowing us to state the extent to which a given person's expectations are (un)justified. The literature sometimes speaks in such cases of unrealistic absolute optimism (Shepperd et al., 2013).

Second, we can explore unrealistic optimism in a manner similar to how the occurrence of the previously discussed better-than-average effect is operationalized, namely, at the group (vs. individual) level. A similar process occurs with regard to unrealistic optimism: people can be asked to determine the probability that they will experience various desirable and undesirable events in their lives and to determine the probability that the same things will happen to the average person. If it is the case that most people believe their chances of positive experiences are higher than the average person, while their chances of having negative experiences are lower, we are observing unrealistic optimism at the group level. We may speak of an internal censor falsifying the probability of events while not claiming that it applies to every individual. In contrast to unrealistic absolute optimism, we can call this phenomenon unrealistic comparative optimism (Shepperd et al., 2013).

Let's start with the first of these issues. In some cases, the unrealistic nature of positive expectations about the future can be ascertained only after the event in question has occurred. Thus, for example, it is possible to determine students' realism or unrealism about their grade on an exam only after they have taken it (e.g., Ruthig et al., 2017) or the degree of unrealism of their optimism about the salary they will receive after graduation by confronting their prior expectations with the offer they actually receive (Shepperd et al., 1996). When it comes to financial advisors, it is also possible to verify post facto the accuracy of their positive expectations about economic developments (Calderon, 1993), and in the case of managers, it is possible to determine whether they were correct in claiming that risky and presently loss-making business projects will prove profitable in the long term (Meyer, 2014). Perhaps the most spectacular effect associated with optimism framed in this way is the planning fallacy. People embarking on a task usually estimate that it will take them less time than it actually subsequently takes (Tversky & Kahneman, 1974). The results of many empirical studies have unequivocally proven this regularity for a wide variety of tasks (e.g., Koole & Spijker, 2000; Griffin & Buehler, 1999; Byram, 1997).

In other cases, the degree of (un)realism of optimism can be estimated at the stage in which we determine the probability of certain states of affairs. As concerns the chances of winning the lottery, it can be precisely calculated. Thus, if someone filling out a lottery ticket believes that they have a better chance of winning than the math would indicate, we can safely call this optimism unrealistic. Similarly, someone who pulls out 1 of 52 cards from the deck, hoping to draw the ace of spades, believes that they have, say, a ten or even five percent chance of drawing that very card demonstrates completely unjustified, and therefore unrealistic, optimism (Marks, 1951; Irwin, 1953).

In other cases, we cannot rely on such clear-cut calculations derived from probability calculus but can rely on approximations. With precise data on the patient's condition, his medical history, data on genetic burdens, etc., a doctor or insurer can, based on a computer algorithm, determine the approximate probability of the patient's recovery or calculate how long the patient is likely to live. If the patient's expectations deviate significantly toward more positive illusions (longer life expectancy) than these estimates, we can term this optimism unrealistic.

This operationalization of unrealistic optimism may seem appropriate, since we relate it to a specific person (e.g., someone has "good" vs. "bad" genes and a long vs. short life in the family) who either is or is not unrealistically optimistic and not – as is the case with comparative optimism – to a group of people, some of whom may be realistically optimistic and only some of whom demonstrate unfounded optimism (not everyone should not assume that they will live longer than others). In fact, however, the issue is far more complex. Indeed, in psychological research, unrealistic optimism has rarely been estimated in the manner outlined above, and so the whole battery of variables related to a person's life history, genetic, and personality factors affecting their current and future situation, etc. has rarely been taken into account. In general, the estimates made by participants were compared with the probability of certain states of affairs in a population. The respondents thus made judgments about how likely it was that they would have breast cancer or the likelihood that they would need to undergo dental surgery; it was then checked how far these judgments deviated from the probabilities calculated for the population to which, demographically speaking, the given person belonged (e.g., Hanoch et al., 2019, 2022).

By the same token, a specific individual who believes, for example, that their likelihood of contracting lung cancer is significantly less than would result from statistics that take into account the incidence of smokers of their sex and age may simply be right. This is because their estimates take into account the fact that there has never been a case of cancer in their family, and they may reasonably assume that by not smoking they are avoiding this serious disease. Similarly, someone who would estimate a lower probability of causing a car accident than the statistics would indicate may be right, either because they are a very experienced and cautious driver who hasn't received a ticket in twenty years or because they don't drive, thereby excluding the possibility of causing an accident. In fact, the factors that individual participants may take into account that objectively modify the probability of a variety of desirable and undesirable events are abundant, and it is downright impossible to take them all into account when calculating a probability that we might deem objective.

Therefore, we feel that a more appropriate way to study unrealistic optimism is through a procedure in which people compare themselves to other people. While we do not know whether, in the case of a particular individual manifesting optimism, this optimism is of an unrealistic nature, it should be explicitly emphasized that we also do not assume that we know this. On the contrary, we talk about the unrealistic nature of optimism exclusively at the group level because "everyone can't have a greater chance than the average person" (in the case of positive events) and "everyone can't have a lesser chance than the average person" (in the case of negative events).

Before proceeding to a discussion of the regularities associated with unrealistic optimism understood from this perspective, let us emphasize that studies which simultaneously measure absolute optimism and comparative optimism have shown that they are distinct phenomena, in the sense that it is possible for one to manifest absolute optimism while not manifesting comparative optimism, and vice versa – i.e., manifesting comparative optimism, in the absence of absolute optimism. The dynamics of change over time of the two types of unrealistic optimism may also differ (Ruthig et al., 2017).

The first studies on comparative unrealistic optimism were carried out by the creator of the concept, Neil Weinstein (1980). He asked students to estimate how likely they were to experience 18 positive states of affairs in the future (such as "like postgraduation job," "owning your own home," "living past 80," or "having a mentally gifted child") and 22 negative states of affairs (such as "having a drinking problem," "attempting suicide," "heart attack before age 40," or "being sterile"), compared to the average student of their sex from their university. They were instructed to specify the difference in percentages (from 0, meaning no possibility of occurrence, to 100, meaning completely certain occurrence of a given event), indicating the direction of the difference. In the vast majority of cases the students were convinced that desirable things would happen to them rather than to others, while undesirable things would happen to others rather than to them.

Surely you have noticed, presenting the results of Weinstein's (1980) pioneering study, that unrealistic optimism was very pronounced for some future possible states of affairs (e.g., like postgraduation job or having a drinking problem) and weaker for others (e.g., having a mentally gifted child or having gum problems). There were also categories for which the phenomenon of unrealistic optimism was not noted (e.g., marrying someone wealthy or being a victim of burglary). Weinstein's explanation is that optimistic distortions (biases) are particularly fostered by events that the individual perceives as controllable. People may, for example, believe that they will choose the kind of job they like, but whether they will be robbed depends more on the burglar than on themselves. (Moreover, if they simultaneously believe that they will earn well, they should, after all, also consistently assume that a burglar will want to break into their house rather than the house of a poorer neighbor.) In turn, this should diminish their optimism about the possibility of avoiding an unwanted visit from a burglar. Also, some diseases and unfortunate events are of such a nature that, at least at some point in one's life, they can be avoided (e.g., alcoholism or drowning in a pool if one cannot swim and does not enter pools), while the occurrence of others is influenced much less or, practically speaking, not at all (e.g., pancreatic cancer or being hit by a car).

At the same time, Weinstein states unequivocally that the optimistic nature of such judgments that he has revealed is not necessarily unrealistic for all people questioned. Undoubtedly, some students have perfectly rational grounds for believing, for example, that they will own their own home (because they have, e.g., rich parents who have promised them this) or that they will most likely manage to avoid a heart attack before the age of 40 (because no one in their family has ever had heart trouble and they themselves are not obese, play recreational sports, eat healthily, do not smoke, drink alcohol only occasionally and in small amounts, undergo regular checkups frequently, and avoid a stressful lifestyle). However, unrealistic optimism can be considered at the group level, because it is simply mathematically impossible for most people to have a better chance of experiencing positive states and avoiding negative states than the average person.

Subsequent empirical research on unrealistic comparative optimism has confirmed that with regard to a great many future events, people believe that positive events are more likely to happen to them than to others and that negative events are more likely to happen to others than to themselves. This research not only confirmed the results obtained in Weinstein's (1980) pioneering study but also revealed other areas in which people feel a specific kind of privilege. Thus, it is others (rather than me) who will fall victim to various types of crime (Perloff & Fetzer, 1986); it is others (rather than me) who will be involved in a serious car accident (McKenna, 1993); it is other women (rather than me) who will experience an unwanted pregnancy (Burger & Burns, 1988). Also, study participants tended to reveal a strong conviction that various illnesses and ailments (not just those studied in Weinstein's pioneering study) would befall other people in the future, rather than themselves (Clarke et al., 2000; Hoorens & Buunk, 1993; Weinstein, 1983, 1984, 1987). Perhaps the most spectacular example of comparative unrealistic optimism came from a survey of pilots. As many as 95% of them were convinced that another, average pilot was more likely to cause an airplane accident in the future than they were (O'Hare, 1990).

The hypothesis that unrealistic optimism is stronger with respect to controllable events than those over which the participant has minimal or no influence on their occurrence (or avoidance in the case of negative events) has also found support in other, more contemporary studies (e.g., Harris, 2008; Klein & Helweg-Larsen, 2002; Menon et al., 2009). In one of them, the belief of having influence turned out to be so strongly linked to unrealistic optimism that it led Dutch prostitutes to believe that they were less likely to contract AIDS than the average Dutch woman (van der Velde et al., 1994). Other research has shown, in turn, that people very often believe that others have less influence on achieving desirable states and avoiding undesirable ones than they do themselves (Hoorens & Smits, 2001), which also strongly supports the thesis of a positive relationship between beliefs about personal control (already referred to more than once) and the degree of unrealistic optimism.

A second factor that largely determines the very occurrence of the unrealistic optimism effect (and, possibly, its magnitude) is the degree to which the occurrence of a particular event is important to the individual. Having an interesting and, in addition, well-paid job is important both from an existential, long-term perspective and from a self-esteem perspective. The fact that someone can steal our car (especially if it is insured against theft) is far less important particularly in the long run (except, perhaps, when one makes a living from driving; but that is, after all, the exception to the rule, certainly only a small number of those reading this work are professional drivers). Such an event would not be a great blow to our existence, and self-esteem is unlikely to be affected at all. Not surprisingly, with regard to work after graduation, unrealistic optimism was very pronounced, while with regard to the possibility of losing one's car, the effect was entirely absent.

It is also easy to see that, in general, unrealistic optimism is more pronounced for negative events than for positive ones. This is an effect consistent with a regularity that stems from prospect theory (Kahneman & Tversky, 1979). Avoiding losses is usually more important to people than achieving gains. Congruently, people are more motivated to believe that something bad will happen to other people rather than to them than they are to believe that something good will happen to them rather than to other people.

Finally, it is worth asking not only whether the effect exists (we have already answered this) but also what purpose it serves. What psychological mechanisms constitute the phenomenon of unrealistic optimism? As with the better-than-average effect discussed earlier, motivations related to protecting and elevating self-esteem (self-protection and self-enhancement) underlie comparative unrealistic optimism. In the case of unrealistic optimism about adverse events, however, we can also refer to a reduction in fear of the future that was not present in BTAE. Unrealistic optimism allows us not to worry about what might happen (Hoorens, 1995; Klein & Weinstein, 1997), deceiving ourselves about the fact that although the given "bad" events happen, they do not happen to me: the person who engages in these falsifications. It is easier, for example, to get in the car and drive to a family reunion believing that traffic accidents will happen to other people rather than to me, allowing us to take the wheel with less anxiety/less fear. Similarly, we may deceive ourselves when considering whether to grab a beer, believing that alcoholism threatens other people rather than us. Absent such optimistic beliefs, driving could be associated with tremendous stress, and drinking beer would not be an enjoyable experience.

In the case of the better-than-average effect, mechanisms of a cognitive nature played a significant role. It is no different with regard to unrealistic optimism. Recall that in BTAE, we noted that in the case of future events that can be influenced in some way, individuals are much more aware of their own competence and their own actions that they plan to engage in, rather than the competence and behavior planned by others. One's own actions are simply almost always cognitively available (the actor is aware of them), while the actions of others are only sometimes available. Thus, an individual may mistakenly believe that they manifest certain behaviors more often than others or those behaviors are more relevant or properly adjusted to the external environment than others. This mechanism is usually referred to by psychologists as cognitive egocentrism. (We note in passing that individuals should also realize to a greater extent that they themselves are more likely than others to manifest inappropriate behavior, such as risky behavior. This, in turn, should not facilitate the appearance of the unrealistic optimism effect. Cognitive egocentrism thus has some limitations as a mechanism for explaining the occurrence of the illusion discussed here, which is usually overlooked in the psychological literature.)

Another cognitive mechanism responsible for falsification or self-deception may be those related to attentional focus. It may already be obvious to you that in the case of comparisons with other people, individuals are focused on themselves – we serve as our own target, or reference point. However, if we ask someone to first estimate the probability of a certain event occurring in the life of another, (average) person, we will focus their attention on that very social object. Now it is this object ("average person") that will be the target or referent point, which may weaken cognitive egocentrism. It has emerged that in such a situation, the power of unrealistic optimism diminishes (e.g., Chambers et al., 2003; Hoorens, 1995). Our focus of attention then shifts from the "inner falsifier/censor" to other people. Still other cognitive mechanisms conducive to the emergence of comparative unrealistic optimism have been written about extensively, e.g., Chambers and Windschitl (2004) and Shepperd et al. (2013).

Despite many similarities, the two comparative distortions (biases) described in this chapter differ in more than just the aforementioned element: better than average refers to constants, e.g., features, while UO refers to events in the future. Besides, the better-than-average effect and unrealistic optimism bias are distinct in that both mechanisms may be present in a specific situation but only one may be present in another situation. For example, the unrealistic optimism bias is present, and the better-than-average effect is not when a person thinks: "I am not better than others, but I have always had a lot of luck in my life" or "I believe God will save me from misfortune."

At the same time, however, the similarities between the two phenomena are quite striking. We should emphasize that both in the case of the better-than-average effect and comparative unrealistic optimism, we are dealing with the favoritism of one's own self in the processes of social comparison, while the object of these comparisons is not some specific other person but a set of people, belonging to the same group as the subject. In other words, as a censor working for ourselves, we falsify – in a positive way – our self-image, our actions, and the future that awaits us. Another issue binding these two concepts is their illusionality: the judgments are not grounded in facts and are impossible from a logical point of view. They are impossible since half should perceive themselves as better and the other half as worse. Not surprisingly, in the literature on the subject, the two phenomena are often discussed together (e.g., Chambers & Windschitl, 2004; Helweg-Larsen & Shepperd, 2001). In the next chapter, we will combine the knowledge discussed here so far with the purpose of this book: we will inquire whether these falsifications also take place during pandemics. If so, how do they manifest themselves? And if they do manifest themselves, how do they affect health-promoting behavior: do they help cope with a pandemic or, just the opposite, do they accelerate the falsifier's destruction by risking illness and even death? And finally, we will consider whether changes are possible, "psychological vaccines" for the disease to reduce harmful illusions.

We will begin with a presentation of research with these comparative biases during the specific time of the spread of the disease, which in 2019 in China was initially diagnosed as severe pneumonia and which in the following year took the form of the COVID-19 pandemic, haunting almost the entire world by evoking such notions as pandemic (rather than epidemic), mass death, and helplessness.

Chapter 2
How Did We Forge a Bearable Reality in COVID-19? Biases in Social Comparative Judgments in a Time of Pervasive Threat

2.1 Dynamics of Unrealistic Optimism in a Time of Pervasive Threat

In the previous chapter, we presented research on comparative biases: better than average and unrealistic optimism. These biases have proven to be widespread and strong, and the studies in which they were revealed have been replicated many times. It is worth noting, however, that these studies were conducted in situations (unrealistic optimism, UO) and general characteristics (better-than-average effect, BTAE) that can be described in the simplest terms as typical, or common: getting cancer, having a car accident, getting a lower-paying job, or experiencing unemployment. However, in human life, at least in some lives, there are situations that prove surprising and threatening to a very large portion of the population. Such events can include both natural disasters, such as floods, earthquakes, fires covering huge areas, volcanic eruptions, hurricanes, or locust plagues, and man-made disasters, such as wars, nuclear power plant disasters, or acts of terror such as the two planes hitting the World Trade Center towers. The question arises whether in just such conditions, where the threat is new and at the same time pervasive, people also feel privileged when they compare their threat with that of others who find themselves in analogous conditions. In such emergencies, do we also introduce a censor falsifying our world to make it more bearable, or even optimistic?

There is very little research on this issue. This is because most such events occur completely unexpectedly, and as a result, psychologists are unable to prepare their studies in advance. After all, psychologists didn't know that terrorists would attack the World Trade Center or that Russia would attack Ukraine, and news of impending tragedies such as a tsunami, the bursting of a dam on a major river, or a hurricane usually comes only hours ahead of the actual occurrence of the tragedy. There is, however, anecdotal data in situations where the research apparatus has been prepared and studies conducted during such acute events.

W. Kulesza, D. Doliński, *Social Biases During Covid 19*, SpringerBriefs in Psychology, https://doi.org/10.1007/978-3-031-34706-1_2

So when, on the night of April 25–26, 1986, the reactor core overheated at the Chernobyl nuclear power plant (in what was then the Soviet Union, today Ukraine), followed by a hydrogen explosion and the spread of radioactive substances over a growing area, psychologists managed to react in time. This is because the cloud containing radioactive substances moved relatively slowly to the north and west of Europe. This made it possible to study the phenomenon of unrealistic optimism in Poland (Ukraine's western neighbor, which was the first to be affected by the contamination; our place of birth and residence), even before the radioactive cloud reached that country.

One of the authors of this book – Dariusz Doliński – together with colleagues (Doliński et al., 1987) observed that the effect of unrealistic optimism previously noted by psychologists in cases where the threats about which the respondents were asked concerned individual people (a heart attack affects one person, as does cancer, a traffic accident affects at most a few people) rather than large populations (it is not the case that a mass of people or a whole society suddenly has a heart attack, gets cancer, or has an accident). Moreover, the Polish researchers pointed out that, to date, the threat had been of a prospective, rather than real nature: hitherto, a hypothetical onset of cancer or the occurrence of a hypothetical traffic accident had been analyzed. After all, cancer victims or accidents had not been studied. Finally, to date, known rather than unknown phenomena had been analyzed, e.g., becoming an alcoholic or a victim of a burglary, losing one's job, or dying in a train crash is predictable; no one predicts a nuclear power plant explosion or a terrorist attack on the WTC until they happen. For this reason, it is difficult to study and measure something that is not there and cannot even be predicted. This time, the researchers wondered what would happen with unrealistic optimism, whether it would also appear in conditions where the threat is widespread, real, current, and entirely novel. All of these conditions were met by the radioactive contamination that was looming over Poland (the country where we live and experienced this tragedy): it was sudden, it had never occurred before – making it unpredictable – and it affected the entire population. For this reason, we also take a look at this unique study because COVID-19 and our research that we present in this book deal with a very similar situation: mass, unpredictable, threatening events. The possibility of falling ill as a result of elevated radioactivity, which was expected to increase dramatically in the coming days, is, from this perspective, very similar to the possibility of contracting COVID-19, where the probability escalates as the pandemic develops.

The radioactive cloud reached Opole, a 100,000-strong university town in southwestern Poland, on April 30, 1986. Studies on unrealistic optimism were conducted a few days later – on May 5 – at a time when contamination was still ongoing due to the breadth of the cloud. Residents of this city, university students, were asked to compare the likelihood of them and the average student of their sex experiencing various potential negative events of a predictable, individual nature: getting cancer, experiencing a heart attack, being the victim of a burglary in their own home, or being the victim of a traffic accident. Here we noted, repeatedly found in psychological research and discussed in detail by us in the previous chapter, the effect of unrealistic optimism. Our participants thought that the bad things mentioned would happen to others rather than to them.

However, and of particular importance, the participants were also asked to compare the probabilities of contracting radiation sickness (i.e., a sudden, unknown, current event, rather than one that may occur in the nebulous future) over the next month, year, and 5 years, relative to themselves and the average student at this university of their sex (the question of sex will return in our present research on COVID-19). While the two measures did not differ too strongly when they estimated the probability of getting sick within the next month, for the longer term (1 year and especially 5 years), the two estimates already differed markedly. Crucially, however, most of the participants considered themselves more likely to get sick than the average student. So it was quite different from previous studies of unrealistic optimism, in which people compare a threat to themselves with a threat to others. We called this effect unrealistic pessimism, because, to reiterate, an inverted trend was noted: the respondents considered themselves more threatened! In the next chapter, we will return to this research in a new context by showing unrealistic optimism and pessimism in the context of whether they help maintain health or ruin it.

We note here at once what we have already emphasized several times above in discussing BTAE and UO: this bias, too, can only be spoken of in a group sense, not in an individual sense. This is because, no doubt, some people may have had rational reasons for believing that they were particularly vulnerable to getting sick: they often went outside, subjecting themselves to more radiation emanating from the radioactive cloud, or they could not give up drinking fresh milk (which, as a result of contaminated feed, must have contained radiation), etc. However, if a clear majority considers itself more vulnerable to radiation sickness than the average other, this is – from a logical or mathematical perspective – just as impossible as the unrealistic optimism or better-than-average optimism we have analyzed earlier.

In order to confirm the existence of a new phenomenon or disprove it (it is always possible that a given study was conducted on a unique sample of people, a different continent, conducted in a different culture of a communist country, the analyzed event was unique and does not replicate with other sudden, massive and unpredictable events, etc.), a few years later, Burger and Palmer (1992) decided to use an event that took place in 1989. This was the earthquake in California, which, from the perspective of interest here, was very similar to the Chernobyl nuclear power plant explosion: it was new, unexpected, and therefore surprising; it was unknown if and when it would come; and it affected an entire society on an unprecedented scale. As in our study, 3 days after the tragic earthquake occurred, researchers asked people how likely they were to become victims of a similar natural disaster in the future and how likely it was to happen to another average person. It turned out that in this case, too, the people surveyed revealed unrealistic pessimism, indicating the universality of the claim that in such situations people think of themselves as more vulnerable than the average person. Burger and Palmer (1987), however, went a step further and repeated this research 3 months after the aforementioned tragic event. As it turned out, the pattern of results this time was very different! People now

Table 2.1 Mean likelihood estimates for being seriously hart in a natural disaster, such as an earthquake

Time of estimate	Self	Average student	Average person
Three days after the earthhquake	3.71	3.50	3.46
Three months after the Earthhquake	2.79	3.32	3.37

Source: *Personality and Social Psychology Bulletin, 14*, p. 42
Copyright: SAGE
Note: Estimates could range from 1 to 7, higher numbers indicating greater perceived likelihood

demonstrated a distinct unrealistic optimism: they believed that an earthquake was more likely to happen to someone else than to them (see Table 2.1). Interestingly, an analogous return of (unrealistic) optimism also occurred a few weeks after the explosion of the Chernobyl power plant (Dolinski & Gromski, 1987), when the majority of students demonstrated the belief that others, rather than them, would fall ill in the future from diseases caused by elevated radioactivity.

This means that the workings of the falsifying internal censor can be multifarious (the issue of stability over time of comparative illusions will return in subsequent chapters, where we will present studies in which we tested changes in cognitive biases in the context of the sudden and unknown threat emanating from the COVID-19 pandemic).

Before proceeding further (approaching the analysis of cognitive biases in the COVID-19 pandemic), let us briefly summarize the three phenomena described: better than average, unrealistic optimism, and unrealistic pessimism. Everything appears to indicate that the normal (typical) state is a positive illusion, which allows people not to experience constant anxiety and not to worry about their own uncertain future. However, if there is a sudden, unexpected, and widespread threat, such an illusion could be dangerous, because it would prevent people from taking actions aimed at avoiding this threat or, if that is not possible, at least at limiting its negative effects (as we write more about in Sect. 3.1 showing that pessimism evoked a healthy, active desire to protect one's own health). As it turns out, under the influence of experiencing anxiety, people's positive optimistic illusions disappear. Dewberry and Richardson (1990) studied their students either in a neutral situation or just before a difficult and important exam. Obviously, in the latter situation, the students were experiencing anxiety (which, by the way, the researchers verified with the help of self-report surveys). It turned out that in a state of anxiety, the participants ceased believing that they were less vulnerable than others to various negative events, such as being mugged or having an obesity-induced heart attack. Helweg-Larsen (1999), on the other hand, demonstrated the absence of positive illusions after people experienced the 1994 California earthquake. Apparently, this was a very powerful experience for those who lived through it, because even 5 months after the event just thinking about it caused such pronounced anxiety that the effect of unrealistic optimism was still not present.

Fortunately for us as a society, events such as the nuclear power plant explosion (1986), the California earthquake (1989), and the terrorist attack on the World Trade Center in New York (2001), unexplored at the time in the context of unrealistic optimism, took place decades ago, sparing us from experiencing similar tragedies. The absence of such negative events is – fortunately! – trouble for scientists who, wishing to study the cognitive biases that falsify reality in the case of such tragedies, have no field, no theater to study, and no material to publish. Of course, it is not as if scientists are waiting longingly for such tragedies to occur. However, if they do occur, they become an opportunity to conduct unique research. The emergence of the coronavirus pandemic in 2019 provided just such a situation.

Therefore, one could expect that the previously presented full dynamics of comparative judgments (from unrealistic pessimism to optimism) would be present with regard to the coronavirus pandemic, as it fulfilled all the criteria of the Chernobyl nuclear explosion situation and the California earthquake: it was sudden, unknown, affected the entire population, and concerned the present (and not the future as is the case with most studies of unrealistic optimism, the probabilities of heart attack, alcoholism, or cancer). We expected that in the first phase, when people were just anticipating that the pandemic would also appear in their country, they would react with pronounced unrealistic pessimism. Over time, this effect would diminish, followed by unrealistic optimism, which would continue throughout. The looming deadly tragedy also opened up further areas that had not yet been explored. For example, is it possible to modify unrealistic optimism? Is it beneficial – does it encourage vaccination? Or, by falsifying reality, does it calm us and reduce stress, but at the same time does it do harm by causing us, like the Titanic, to wash over an iceberg sunk in a blissful fog of intoxicating positive thinking? The answers to questions may be crucial to predicting human behavior during any future pandemics or other sudden, large-scale emergencies.

During the COVID-19 pandemic, we wanted to test a new, hitherto unexplored falsification of reality by scrutinizing the functioning of the censor, who had to confront an influx of unambiguous epidemiological data and explicit media messages. Note that if there is not a single case of a given infectious disease in a given area, it is reasonable to assume that a given social group believes that the risk of contracting the disease is low. For example, it is difficult to expect Poles, Americans, or Australians to fear the localized, yet highly contagious and dangerous, Ebola virus. Using the research experience one of us obtained from studying the radioactive contamination that resulted from the Chernobyl power plant accident, we decided to capture in our research the moment before the actual threat of contamination and the moment of the advent of the threat and, moreover, to look at how the dynamics of comparative judgments change as the threat becomes progressively greater.

In our first study, we captured the initial phase of the threat by conducting measurements of unrealistic expectations (we deliberately avoid unrealistic optimism, as we could not exclude the possibility that unrealistic pessimism would follow) before reports of the diagnosis of the first case of COVID-19 in Poland (i.e., the country where we conducted this research; Dolinski et al. 2020). We make no secret of the fact that we were quite lucky in doing so, since the first phase of our research on the student population took place on March 2 and 3, 2020, while the government notified Polish citizens of the first identified case the following day (March 4). So we captured the moment of analyzing a risk when it did not yet exist in a particular region of the world. Importantly, our research continued. We thus decided to study a different group of people immediately after the aforementioned press release (i.e., on March 5 and 6). In the following days, there were new reports of COVID-19 cases, illustrating the rapid spread of the disease throughout the country. This prompted us to conduct the next phase of the study on March 9 and 10. In doing so, we intended to conduct successive waves of research, but because of the pandemic situation, all Polish universities were closed. Thus, the possibility of engaging students was limited.

It is worth explaining at this point that we decided to use a slightly different procedure for determining the level of unrealistic pessimism/optimism than Weinstein (1980) did in his pioneering research. This is because we elected to study the estimation of the risks that the participants believed they were incurring and the risks that they believed the average person was incurring on two separate scales. By doing so, the dynamics of comparative judgments could be more precisely tracked. If, for example, there was an increase in unrealistic optimism over a certain period of time, then, using the methodology we chose, it was possible to determine whether this change was due to the participant's belief that the threat to them had decreased or whether it was due to the fact that the threat to others had increased (or the fact that both processes occurred at the same time). The use of only a single measure, as proposed by Weinstein and often used in studies of unrealistic optimism, does not offer this possibility. If a participant in a study says, for example, that they are less likely to get sick than 75% of the people in their group and 2 weeks later estimates that they are less likely to get sick than 90% of such people, we will know that their level of optimism has increased, but we will not know what the nature of the change is. Did our respondent feel more secure on their own, did they judge that others are now more at risk than before, or did both processes occur together? We also made an analogous methodological assumption for all of our other research that we present in this book, enriching the literature on the subject with not only a more accurate measurement but allowing for a more nuanced analysis.

What were the results of our study? Quite unexpectedly for us, there was unrealistic optimism (rather than the unrealistic pessimism we had expected) in the first phase, which was, after all, implemented before the pandemic appeared in Poland. It persisted in the two subsequent measurements as well, that is, when the threat was becoming real and widespread! Since the dynamics of this bias were slightly different for men and women (and again we highlight sex differences, which we will discuss in more detail shortly), in Figs. 2.1 and 2.2, we present the results separately for both sexes.

The student population is certainly quite specific (education, access to expert information, residing in a large city, relatively low age of the participants, life status generally associated with not having to earn a living, often living with parents), and the fact that it is most often studied by psychologists is due solely to the easy accessibility of people from this group to researchers. However, a legitimate question arises: would a similar effect occur with another social group whose characteristics are closer to those of the general population?

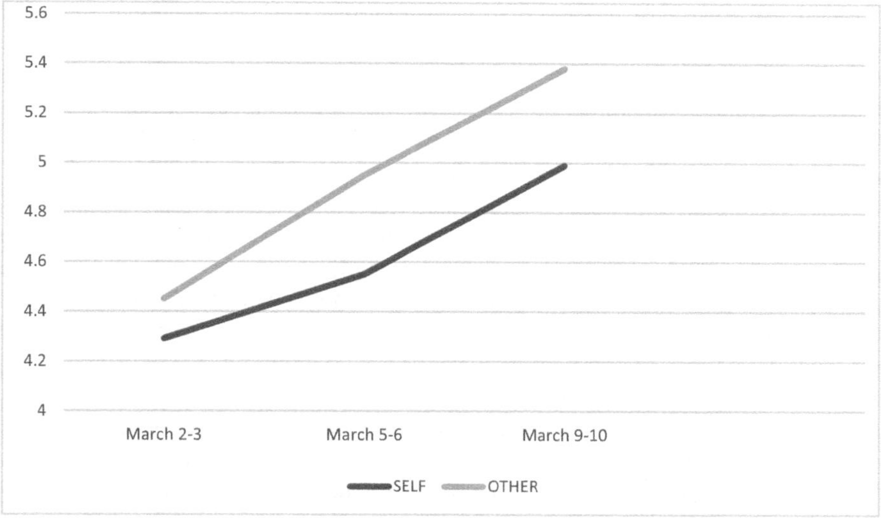

Fig. 2.1 Women's estimates of the likelihood of contracting coronavirus and the likelihood that an average student of the same sex will be infected at three different time intervals
Source: *Journal of Clinical Medicine*, *9*, 1464, Figure 1

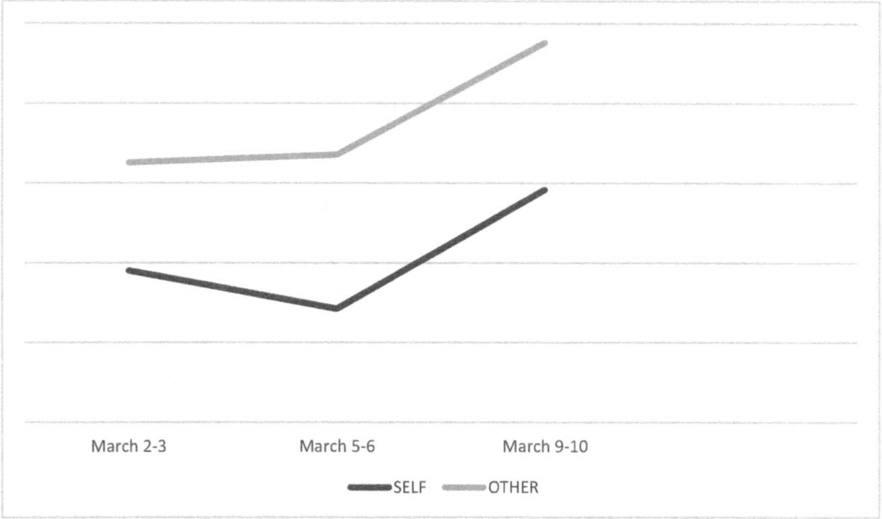

Fig. 2.2 Men's estimates of the likelihood of contracting coronavirus and the likelihood that an average student of the same sex will be infected at three different time intervals
Source: *Journal of Clinical Medicine*, *9*, 1464, Figure 2

As a team, we asked ourselves these questions at about the same time. We decided to approach the employees of a multinational company, and since this time we adopted an online research formula, our study was not interrupted by a lockdown; the study was safe for both the respondents and ourselves, the researchers (who worked remotely); and we could conduct a longitudinal study (12 waves conducted from early March of 2020, when vaccines were unavailable in Poland, through early March of 2021, during the period when vaccines became available) for an extended period of time regardless of changes in external circumstances. Of particular importance is that we conducted our study on the same individuals, so the possibility of (lack of) variability over time could not be attributed to different participants being measured at different intervals. In this case, too, we had time to start the study before the first case of COVID-19 was identified in Poland (Izydorczak et al., 2022). As can be seen in Fig. 2.3, employees of the corporation, like students, also reacted consistently – albeit with varying degrees of intensity – with unrealistic optimism. Replication in two independent studies of the same result thus demonstrates the astonishing strength of the effect we noted: with an influx of objective – and threatening! – information, the falsifying censor continued its work! What's more, these were most likely the world's first studies of unrealistic optimism that examined potential variability over time to demonstrate how stable this effect is.

The aforementioned results and changes in the strength of unrealistic optimism (but not its eradication!) prompted us to investigate post facto what could have caused them. We took two factors into consideration. The first was the objective data on the statistics regularly presented in the media: newly reported cases of COVID-19 and deaths attributable to it. Note that the graph of the number of fatal

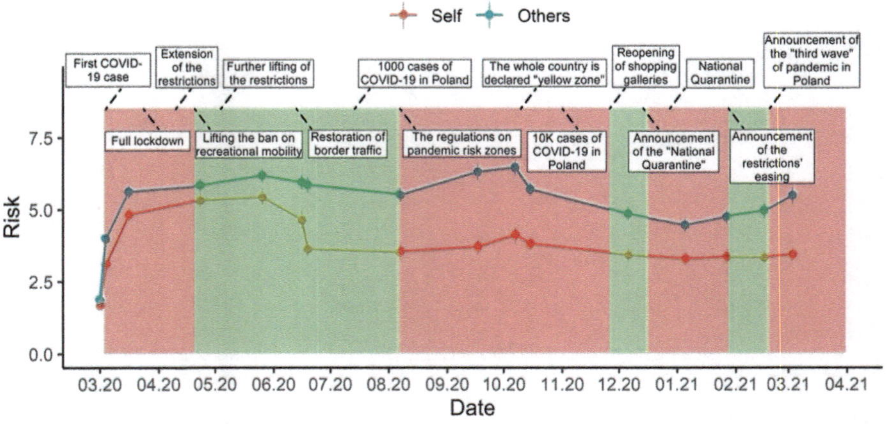

Fig. 2.3 Line plot of changes in risk estimates over time
Source: PLoS ONE 17(12): e0278045, Figure 4
Copyryght: PLOS ONE
Note: Each dot represents mean risk estimates for "Self" (blue) and "Other" (red) at a given time. Bars represent standard errors of means. Frames above the graph describe the most important events in the timeline of the pandemic

cases due to coronavirus infection – which often increases not linearly, but rather as an exponential/quadratic function – clearly communicates a deadly threat, while a steady decrease offers reasonable reassurance that the threat is diminishing.

The second factor that may have influenced the variable intensity of the falsification of reality was the Polish government's decisions to introduce or rescind various restrictions. It could have been the case that the tightening of restrictions on social functioning (closing schools, limiting the number of people in stores, limiting the availability of certain medical services) certainly sent a signal – in the case of an increase in restrictions – of a serious and growing threat; if restrictions were being relaxed, then the clear signal being sent was good news that the threat was being reduced.

The results were astonishing, revealing the sheer dramatic irrationality of our judgments about the threat: the censor was closing its eyes! For it turned out that information on the number of identified cases of new illnesses and deaths was in no way correlated with the level of unrealistic optimism. In other words, such a clear indicator as death, an upsurge in queues at funeral homes, or information that someone in our neighborhood died due to COVID-19 does not have an effect on changes in unrealistic optimism. In contrast, the restrictions that were introduced and withdrawn had a very serious effect on the judgments formulated by participants. When restrictions eased, unrealistic optimism increased; when they escalated, unrealistic optimism decreased (but, we should emphasize, never disappeared completely). Characteristically, the introduction and withdrawal of restrictions mainly changed beliefs about the risk to oneself, and it was this element (rather than the risk to others) that influenced changes in the level of unrealistic optimism. Thus, an important message emerges for policy-makers around health issues: during a pandemic (and perhaps in other sudden global emergencies) the more effective approach is to reduce the scale of falsification of reality by showing changes in the social environment. Various restrictions and limitations are a signal to the public that the situation is dangerous. Unjustified optimism (the illusion that nothing bad will happen) should be abandoned, and the recommendations should be complied with.

During the first wave of the COVID-19 pandemic, studies of unrealistic optimism were also conducted in four different European countries (France, Italy, Switzerland, and the United Kingdom) with a very large sample of a total of 12,378 people (McColl et al., 2022). These surveys were conducted three times: February 12–21, March 11–12, and March 31–April 5, 2020. This made it possible not only to examine unrealistic optimism itself in three different time periods but also to trace the dynamics of this bias from its absolute beginnings to a pandemic reaping a hefty death toll. Interestingly, they found that the level of unrealistic optimism consistently increased in all four countries studied. Taking a closer look at this effect, the researchers found that it was due to the fact that participants thought they themselves were becoming less and less likely to contract the disease, while others were consistently just as likely. A little later, in late April to mid-June 2020 (and thus during the first lockdown announced in Belgium and the Netherlands), research on risk perception was conducted by Vera Hoorens and colleagues (2022). This study, too, found clear unrealistic optimism; taking all this data together shows how strong, robust, and global this social bias is.

The obvious question that arises is why the dynamics of comparative judgments in assessing the future risk of disease are different here than those observed in the aforementioned cases of a nuclear power plant explosion or surviving an earthquake. In particular, why, at the very beginning of the study conducted in Poland (when the first case of the disease in this country had yet to even be announced), no unrealistic pessimism effect was found. We think the critical point here is that people had already been bombarded many weeks earlier in the press with various reports about the pandemic, which was steadily and dynamically spreading around the world. It is highly likely that a conviction taking the form of unrealistic pessimism emerged just then, i.e., a few or perhaps several weeks before the first case of the disease in Poland was announced. By the time we began our study, the comparative pessimism of the participants had already given way to comparative optimism. Of course, this is only a hypothesis that can be neither confirmed nor refuted.

One might ask whether the correlations we have found are not confined to Poland or, somewhat more broadly, to a region of the world directly affected by the Iron Curtain, living for decades under the threat of a nuclear war. Later in this volume, we will show that this is not the case by presenting research from the Americas; now we will present our research conducted both in Poland and outside Europe – in Iran and Kazakhstan (Study #1; Kulesza et al., 2021). Let us emphasize how different the compared countries were. Iran is a country under severe embargoes resulting in a weakened healthcare system and response speed and a country governed by laws derived directly from religion (Islam). Poland, an almost entirely Christian, democratic country, was until recently deprived of some of its rights to self-determination on account of being under the influence of the Soviet Union. Kazakhstan lies more or less between the described extremes. Although Islam is present, it is also no stranger to the influence of other religions. The country was also communist until recently, but with weaker democratic inclinations than Poland. The axis of comparison may also be COVID-19 itself, which hit Iran much harder and faster than Poland or Kazakhstan. Unrealistic optimism emerged and persisted in subsequent waves of research (Izydorczak et al., 2022) in all these populations, with stronger optimism in Asian countries (Iran, Kazakhstan) than in the European country (Poland). This once again demonstrates the robustness of this effect.

It should also be emphasized that this bias has also been found in many other studies conducted in countries around the world (beyond the European continent as well) – e.g., in the United States (Salgado & Berntsen, 2021; Sjastad & Van Bavel, 2021), the United Kingdom (Asimakopoulou et al., 2020; Salgado & Berntsen, 2021), Germany (Kupier-Smith et al., 2021), Brazil (Vieites et al., 2021), Poland (Maksim et al., 2022; Kulesza et al., 2020, 2023a), Portugal (Figueiras et al., 2022), Italy (Druică et al., 2020), and Romania (Druică et al., 2020; Maftei & Petroi, 2022).

At this point, it is worth mentioning an interesting effect demonstrated by Kupier-Smith et al. (2020) who conducted a study on March 16, 2020, in three countries (the United Kingdom, Germany, and the United States). They asked participants not only about the likelihood that they and another average person would become ill with COVID-19 in the next 2 weeks, 2 months, 1 year, and lifetime but also about the likelihood that they would transmit the infection to others if they themselves fell ill. Of course, the researchers also asked about the likelihood that the average person infected with the virus would infect other people. These potentially infected people were divided into specific categories: family members, friends, acquaintances, fellow commuters, and strangers with whom one spends leisure time. It turned out that the study participants believed they would be less likely to infect others than that the disease would be spread by the average person. This belief was manifested in relation to all the categories of "other people" mentioned. Interestingly, the strength of this effect was even greater than the strength of unrealistic optimism regarding the possibility of contracting COVID-19. This means that it is necessary for pandemic managers to take into account unrealistic optimism as a mechanism responsible not only for the increase in infections among those with this falsified worldview but, much more importantly, for the increase in transmissions to others ("I don't get infected, others do")!

A pandemic is not only a threat to our health but also a threat to other aspects of our living situation. People's subjective fear of becoming infected has caused them to avoid visiting restaurants, cafes, bars, pubs, or nightclubs. People were also reluctant to organize weekend trips out of town or holiday tourist trips, which obviously translated into a significant reduction in the number of guests at hotels. The official introduction of lockdown further aggravated the situation for the entire HoReCa (hotels, restaurants, catering) industry. Many food service establishments, motels, and hotels faced bankruptcy, or at least (in more optimistic scenarios) a marked reduction in revenue. This inevitably involved the loss of some or all of the earnings and/or employment of personnel working in this industry. Note how evident the threat situation was. It was both an economic and epidemiological threat: this is a dangerous profession; the government is shutting down this business sector, which is a clear indicator of the danger. This raises the question of whether workers in this particular branch of the economy, particularly affected by the COVID-19 pandemic, are displaying unrealistic optimism about their work situation. Logic would dictate that they should not. They have received far too many signals about the looming danger.

To test this, we asked a group of waiters, cooks, and hotel employees questions about the possibility of losing their jobs due to the pandemic, as well as the chances of the same happening to the average person in their business and to their average fellow countryman (Dolinski et al., 2021). They were also asked what the probability was that the company they work for, an average company in the same industry, and an average company (regardless of industry) would go bankrupt due to the ongoing pandemic. As can be seen in Figs. 2.4 and 2.5, the respondents demonstrate strong unrealistic optimism in all these respects. One particularly striking aspect of their responses is that they seem to overlook the distinctive nature of the HoReCa industry. They feel not only privileged in relation to others from their own company but also in relation to the average person in their country. They also think that their company is less likely to go bankrupt than the average company doing the same business (which makes absolutely no sense, all restaurants in the industry were at risk, and it's impossible that a particular respondent's specific workplace is somehow specially protected!) but also less than the average company engaged in any

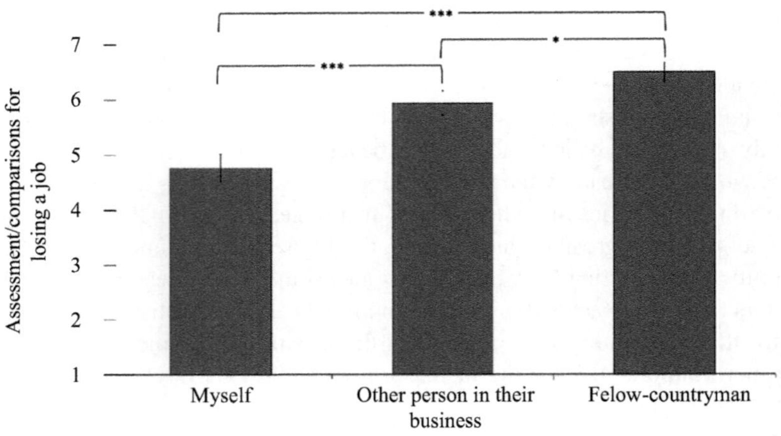

Fig. 2.4 Assesment/comparisons for loosing job
Source: *Sustainability*, *13*, 12562, Figure 3
Copyright: MDPI
Note: Bars represent mean values; error bars represent standard error of mean
$*p < 0.05$; $***p < 0.001$

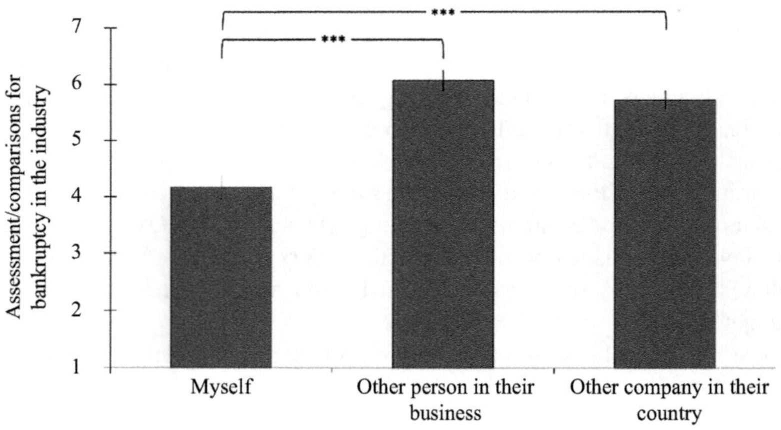

Fig. 2.5 Assesment/comparisons for bankruptcy in the industry
Source: *Sustainability*, *13*, 12562, Figure 4
Copyright: MDPI
Note: Bars represent mean values; error bars represent standard error of mean
$***p < 0.001$

kind of business in their country. Thus, it can be said that – completely contrary to the objective circumstances accessible to this group of workers – they did not think that a pandemic would wreak any particular havoc in specifically the HoReCa industry. In a sense, then, one can conclude that the workers we studied manifested dual positive illusions – about both themselves and the industry that employs them.

As we have repeatedly noted, people in studies on unrealistic optimism compare themselves with those who are similar to them (e.g., students compare themselves with the average student of their sex from their university, people surveyed via online panels with the average user of the panel, employees of a particular company with the average employee of that same company, etc.). Of course, only then can one legitimately employ the term "unrealistic optimism." After all, if, for example, a 20-year-old healthy student believes that they are less likely to be severely affected by COVID-19 than the average resident of their country (and therefore a person much older than them), then, statistically speaking, they are right: they are younger, healthier, and probably from a wealthier home with better access to resources.

For a number of reasons, however, we may also take an interest in situations where people compare themselves not only with the average person from their own group but also with average people from other but similar groups. In one of our studies (Kulesza et al., 2022a), we created just such a situation by extending the circle of comparisons and retaining the previous, classical comparisons to see if the reference point thus measured changes the distribution of results. We conducted this study via the Prolific panel in October 2021, when COVID-19 vaccines were already widely available, with 660 participants from different countries. The participants were compensated financially (GPB 11.50 per hour of activity). As before, the participants were asked a series of questions regarding the probability of various people contracting COVID-19. On a scale of 1 (absolutely impossible) to 11 (quite certain), the respondents determined this probability in relation to themselves, the average Prolific panel user, the average vaccinated Prolific user, and the average unvaccinated Prolific user. Respondents also answered the question of whether they themselves were vaccinated or not.

As for the respondents who were themselves vaccinated, the results were rather predictable. They believed that they were less likely to contract COVID-19 than the average Prolific user, as well as the average vaccinated and unvaccinated user of the platform. At the same time, they believed that the average vaccinated Prolific user was less likely to contract the disease than one who had not been vaccinated. On the other hand, the results regarding participants who had not been vaccinated were remarkably interesting and surprising. They believed that they were less likely to get sick than the average Prolific user and less likely than those users of this panel who had not been vaccinated. Interestingly, however, at the same time, they believed that they were at the same risk of contracting the disease as the average Prolific user who had been vaccinated, while expressing the opinion that a Prolific user who had been vaccinated would become ill with COVID at a lower probability than one who had not been vaccinated. We present the results of this study in Fig. 2.6.

This means, therefore, that those who are unvaccinated grasp the importance of and need for vaccination, but not in relation to themselves. Others who have been vaccinated are therefore, in their – unvaccinated – opinion, in the right, because by doing so they reduce the likelihood of contracting the disease. They themselves, on the other hand, do not need to vaccinate, because even without vaccination they have just as low a risk of getting sick as those who have been vaccinated. This result thus illustrates a triple intellectual Nelson: while being against vaccination, we

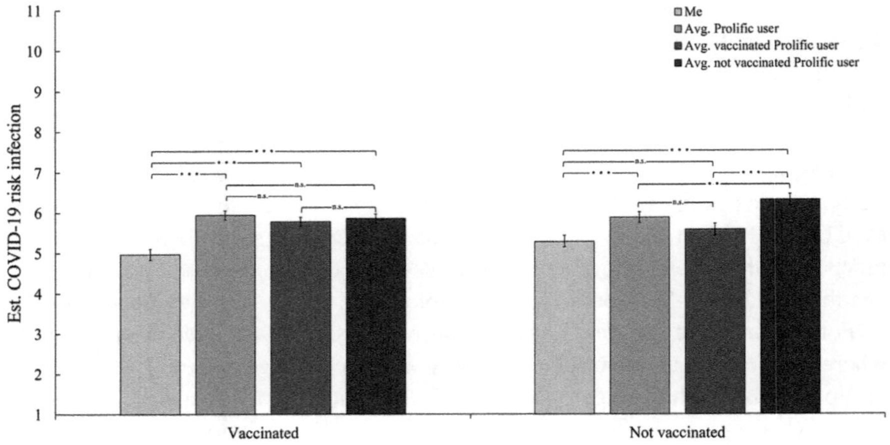

Fig. 2.6 Estimated COVID-19 risk of infection as a function of vaccinated and unvaccinated participants
Source: *Journal of Pacific Rim Psychology, 16.* https://doi.org/10.1177/18344909221122573. Figure 1
Copyright: SAGE
Note: Bars represent mean values; error bars represent standard error of mean
*** $p < 0.001$; ** $p < 0.01$; *ns* not significant ($p > 0.05$)

believe in vaccines – they lower the probability of getting sick. People who do not vaccinate are making a mistake, because they become more likely to get sick. But I am not affected by this correlation: without vaccination I am as immune to getting sick as those who have been vaccinated.

Although we did not investigate this (essentially because we did not expect to see such a shocking result), it is a reasonable supposition that unvaccinated respondents believe that, for some reason (e.g., genetic), they are less likely to get sick than other people. Either way, this entirely unexpected result shows that the decision not to vaccinate oneself is not necessarily the same as a negative assessment of vaccination per se!

Another example of comparing one's chances not only with those of one's own group, but also with those of another group, can be estimating the probability of contracting the disease for oneself, for the average person of the same sex, and for the average person of the other sex. We already know from the various studies reported earlier that most men believe they are less likely to contract COVID-19 than the average man and most women believe they are less likely to contract the disease than the average woman. But will men think they are less at risk than the average woman, and will women believe they are less at risk than the average man?

The issue of such comparisons is interesting insofar as the literature in the field of health psychology contains a wealth of data on cross-sex differences in risk misjudgment (see Byrnes et al., 1999; Courtenay, 2000 for review). This includes, for example, issues such as the consequences of smoking (Weiss & Garbanati, 2006), driving after drinking alcohol (Linkenbach & Perkins, 2005) (see also Dillard et al.,

2009), and the wisdom of undergoing preventive screenings (Mahalik et al., 2006). Of particular relevance from the perspective of interest to us in this book, sex differences were also noted in studies conducted on people's responses during the COVID-19 pandemic, revealing that men were less likely than women to engage in various preventive measures and to follow medical recommendations (e.g., Aranguren, 2022; Lin et al., 2021).

We therefore decided to take a closer look at the topic of comparisons with the average person of the other sex. We conducted three separate studies (in the period from September to November 2021) on a population of American users of the Prolific platform (Kulesza et al., 2023b). These studies differed in several details, but their common feature was that respondents were asked to rate on an 11-point scale the likelihood that they themselves would become ill with COVID-19 and that it would happen to the average Prolific profile user, the average female Prolific user, and the average male Prolific user. The results of the three studies are presented in Table 2.2.

Table 2.2 Risk estimations for all groups in the three individual studies

Study	Gender of the participant	Person of reference	*N*	*M*	*SD*
1	Female	Me	614	4.31	2.07
		Avg. female		5.49	1.79
		Avg. male		5.81	1.84
		Avg. peer		5.51	1.89
	Male	Me	584	4.20	2.39
		Avg. female		5.05	2.22
		Avg. male		5.27	2.21
		Avg. peer		5.15	2.18
2	Female	Me	314	5.61	2.37
		Avg. female		6.10	1.95
		Avg. male		6.46	1.94
		Avg. peer		6.44	1.94
	Male	Me	314	5.32	2.33
		Avg. female		5.97	1.93
		Avg. male		6.05	2.00
		Avg. peer		5.97	2.00
3	Female	Me	315	5.51	2.28
		Avg. female		6.23	2.04
		Avg. male		6.57	2.04
		Avg. peer		6.32	2.01
	Male	Me	314	5.07	2.42
		Avg. female		5.70	2.08
		Avg. male		5.87	2.11
		Avg. peer		5.70	2.10

Source: American Journal of Men's Health, [vol, page]
Copyright: SAGE
Note: *N* number of participants within condition, *M* mean response within group, *SD* standard deviation of response within group

As we can see, both women and men here demonstrate a strong effect of unrealistic optimism (they believe that they are less likely to get sick than the average user of the Prolific platform of their sex), and they also believe that they are less likely to get sick than the average Prolific user of the opposite sex or the average user of the platform regardless of their sex. While the strength of unrealistic optimism was the same for men and women, the participants' beliefs that they are less likely to get sick than the average person of the opposite sex were not equally strong – women were more strongly convinced of this than men.

Let us briefly summarize two recent studies. We note that previous studies on comparative risk estimates have dealt with the comparisons participants make with an average person from their own group. Our studies have shown the presence of a positive illusion effect also when people compared themselves with an average person from another group – vaccinated versus unvaccinated and vice versa, women versus men and vice versa. These results are also relevant to global health policies. They should take into account the universality and strength of positive illusions.

To sum up this section, empirical studies consistently demonstrate that unrealistic optimism is strong and widespread, not only in neutral situations but also during a pandemic. Moreover, it is resistant to clear signals indicating the gravity of the situation (clear and present danger). It is present in all the countries where it was studied, showing that it is not related to the culture or history of a given country nor the background of the study participants.

2.2 The Better-than-Average Effect in a Time of Pervasive Threat

We know from the previous section that unrealistic optimism is at work in the COVID-19 pandemic: research participants from many countries unanimously declare that it is others who will get sick, not them (which, of course, makes no sense; if so many people say they won't get sick, then who will?). Meanwhile, as we already know from Sect. 1.3, unrealistic optimism is not the only means of falsifying reality deployed by the internal censors responsible for our self-image. Another method is the belief that we are, for some reason, better than others. So let's look at whether the censor triggers better-than-average thinking under conditions of a real, massive, and serious threat – during the COVID-19 pandemic.

The first of our studies to address this issue was conducted online on student populations in three countries: Iran, Kazakhstan, and Poland (Kulesza et al., 2022a, b). The surveyed students were asked to indicate on a scale from 1 (do not follow) to 11 (fully follow) to what extent they follow the recommendations just announced in each country for the functioning of daily life during the pandemic. The comparisons involved issues related to the medical recommendations that a given country's citizens can follow to fight the pandemic: wearing masks, maintaining social distance, washing hands frequently with soap and water and disinfecting them, etc. In order to see whether participants see themselves in a better light than other people similar to themselves, we asked them, using the same scale, to declare the extent to which the average student of their sex from their country follows such recommendations and then – in order to estimate the possible magnitude of differences glorifying oneself – to estimate to what extent the average resident of their country does so. We repeated this survey with the same people approximately 10 days later.

As we can see, we registered a classic better-than-average effect. The participants declared that they behaved more correctly than the average student of their sex, and they saw an even greater difference in this regard between themselves and the average resident of their own country. Interestingly, the passage of a mere 10 days reduced the participants' declared belief that they were conscientiously following the recommendations, but similarly, it also reduced it to the same extent for the average student and the average resident of their own country (they, too, according to the respondents, began following the recommendations to a lesser extent than 10 days earlier). Thus, the magnitude of the better-than-average effect remained constant.

An obvious weakness of the above study is that the student population we surveyed is quite specific for many reasons (age, education, place of residence, leisure activities, etc.). A major methodological caveat flows from this finding. It would be unwise to construct recommendations for an entire population on the basis of a study of a specific part of it.

We therefore decided in a subsequent study to examine members of a different population that would be closer to typical average people (Kulesza et al., 2022b, "social psychology journal"). For the study, we selected subscribers to a popular online university newsletter, which features texts and audio broadcasts popularizing scientific knowledge. Since the newsletter appeared in Polish, we were limited to Polish residents. Because of the strict lockdown implemented at the time, the survey was conducted online.

Several hundred such subscribers who agreed to take part in our study were asked – in a similar fashion to the previous survey – first to estimate to what extent they themselves comply with medical recommendations and then to say to what extent they think the average university newsletter subscriber does so; finally, we called on them to estimate the extent to which the average Polish citizen follows such recommendations. As expected, the participants thought they were the ones who behaved the most appropriately; the average newsletter subscriber was less disciplined than them; and the average Pole adhered to the recommendations the least. The better-than-average effect noted in our first study has thus been replicated. Although we still do not have representative data for the entire population, it can already be assumed with greater probability that the pattern of results is typical of residents of the country where we conducted the research (i.e., Poland). However, there is still another problem: perhaps it is only the residents of a particular region of the world who are susceptible to this kind of censorious falsification of reality? In discussing unrealistic optimism, we showed that this is not the case. In the case of better than average, however, further investigations were needed to test the universality of the recorded effects.

Fortunately, studies on the occurrence of the better-than-average effect under pandemic conditions have been conducted in many countries around the world. For example, Kim and Han (2022), surveying 210 respondents from the United States and 214 from South Korea, indicated the prevalence of this effect in both countries; they likewise obtained a result demonstrating the universality of the human tendency to falsify reality. In doing so, the researchers showed that the magnitude of the better-than-average effect correlated with negative attitudes toward people who do not follow medical advice during a pandemic. This result can be interpreted in terms of grievances: "my efforts to stop the pandemic are being thwarted by irresponsible people who totally ignore medical recommendations," which points to a potentially important conclusion for global health practitioners. Think about building narratives aimed at showing the active involvement of a social group in the fight against a pandemic. After all, consider that we have already shown multiple times that the core cognitive biases, the falsification of reality, are comparisons to the group: it is impossible for "everyone to be superior to the average group member." The key, then, may be a narrative about group behaviors to change individuals' perceptions of themselves: you are not necessarily less likely to get sick than others (unrealistic optimism), and you are not necessarily more engaged in protecting yourself than others (better than average). We will return to testing such narratives as a way of curbing the activity of our internal censors, falsifying reality, in Sect. 4.3, where we present a study in which we tested exactly such a method.

Respondents' belief that they behave better, more responsibly, than other people during a pandemic was also tested in European studies conducted in Belgium and the Netherlands (Hoorens et al., 2022). In these studies, participants answered a series of questions on issues such as the medical authorities' recommendation to wash their hands with soap and water more often and more thoroughly than usual and to maintain physical distance from others; they also commented on the frequency of behaviors that are clearly not recommended by medical authorities, such as leaving home for fun, meeting relatives and friends, visiting other people in their homes, and running an errand that is not necessary. The research participants were asked to estimate how often they themselves exhibit such behavior and how often the average person of their age and sex does so. A clear better-than-average effect was noted. Evidently, the Belgians and Dutch they surveyed were convinced that they themselves were more likely to follow medical advice than their fellow countrymen. This effect was particularly pronounced with older (vs. younger) respondents. The researchers also asked the participants about their predictions for the aforementioned behaviors in the near future (how things will be next month). It turned out that while the better-than-average effect also surfaced then, its strength was less.

In doing so, let us note that the predictions of the Belgian and Dutch respondents as the situation in a month's time coincided exactly with the results of the real-time estimation studies we presented above, conducted in Iran, Kazakhstan, and Poland by the first author of this monograph and his colleagues (Kulesza et al., 2022a, b). Perhaps people realize that, under the influence of an emerging threat, they begin to engage in behaviors recommended by authority figures quite intensively, but they habituate existing threats relatively quickly, and the aforementioned avoidance-oriented activities decrease in intensity. This hypothesis may give rise to further practical recommendations. Perhaps changes in narratives that reduce the sense of being superior are needed to avoid weakening the impact of such messages in the long term.

Very interesting results linked to the better-than-average effect (and providing further evidence that the better-than-average effect is not restricted to just one country or residents of one area of Europe) were obtained by Salgado and Berntsen in a study conducted on the UK population (Salgado & Berntsen, 2021). They asked participants about the likelihood in various situations that they would buy and wear masks, use hand sanitizers, and maintain physical distance from others and the likelihood that such behaviors would be exhibited by close others and acquaintances. They also asked questions about the extent to which it is necessary for themselves and close others and acquaintances to manifest these very behaviors in order to effectively guard against the threat of infection. It turned out that, in the respondents' estimation, it is equally necessary for everyone to manifest the aforementioned behaviors, but they themselves exhibit them at a slightly higher frequency than close others, and at a significantly higher frequency than acquaintances – see Fig. 2.7.

The better-than-average effect was also revealed by Kupier-Smith et al. (2020), surveying 828 people from additional European countries (the United Kingdom and Germany) and the United States in March 2020. The participants expressed the belief that they take pandemic-related medical recommendations more seriously and responsibly than the average person. In particular, they believe that they reduce the number of direct interpersonal contacts to a greater extent than other people and are more careful than others about personal hygiene during this exceptional period. And here arises a practical conclusion analogous to the one we presented when discussing the research by Kim and Han (2022). In cases of ubiquitous threats, it seems sensible to make people realize that ... it's simply impossible! As we have previously noted, we are afflicted by cognitive egocentrism: we are more aware of our own actions than of other people's behavior. This causes us to falsify our self-image and that of others. Perhaps, then, active presentation of other people's health-promoting actions in various media could reduce this cognitive bias. We will return to this issue in Chap. 4 with a thorough presentation of a study directly dedicated to this very issue.

The results presented in this chapter clearly indicate that we (i.e., people) believe that we are better than others about following medical recommendations designed to protect us from coronavirus. Thus, we manifest the classic illusion of a better-than-average effect. Not surprisingly, we consequently have a sense of being less likely to contract COVID-19, so we manifest another classic illusion in the form of unrealistic optimism. In other words, it is clear that we defend ourselves against an uncontrollable threat that is challenging to understand by employing a set of cognitive biases: they are double-edge swords cutting in unison, coherently, in multiple directions.

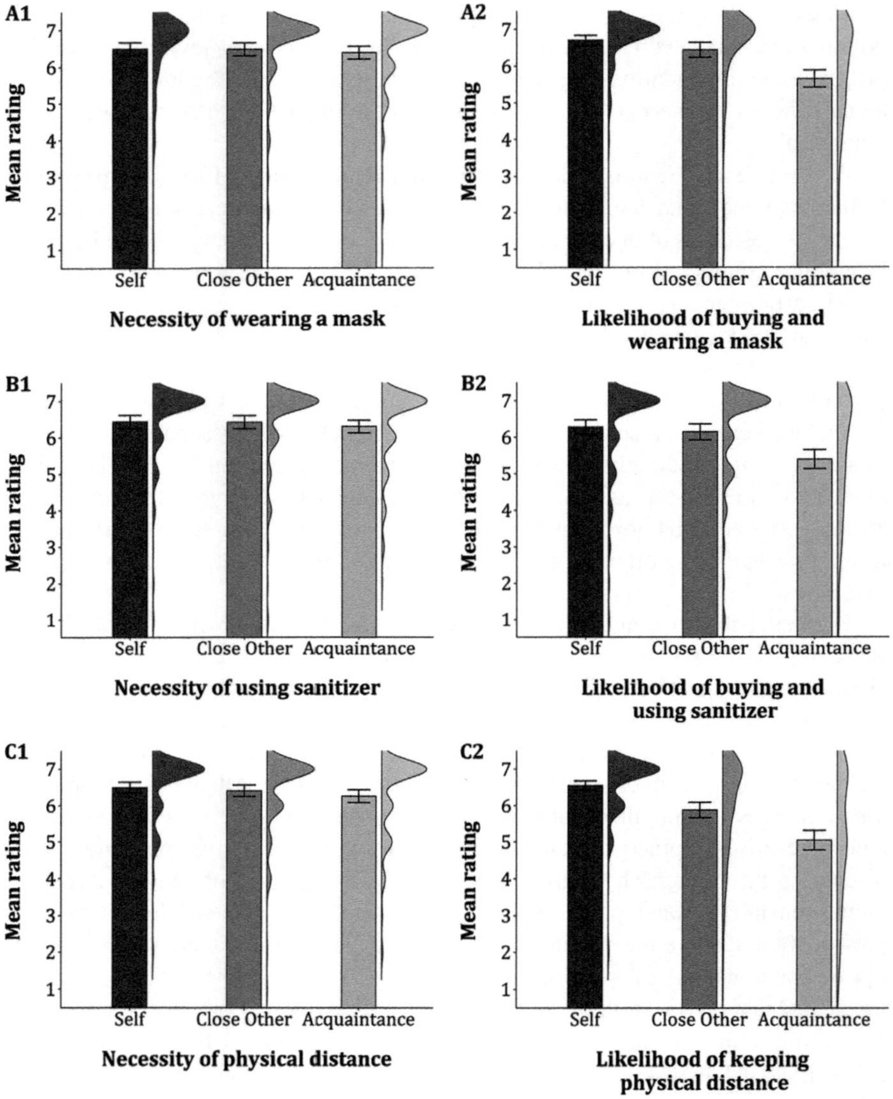

Fig. 2.7 Attitudes towards protective behaviour against COVID-19
Source: *Journal of Applied Research in Memory and Cognition 10*, p. 373
Copyright: Elsevier
Note: Left panels illustrate the necessity of using facemasks (A1), hand sanitizer (B1), and keeping a physical distance (C1). Right panels show the likelihood of buying and using facemasks (A2), hand sanitizer (B2), and the likelihood of keeping a physical distance (C2). All panels illustrate the data as a function of the target of the tasks: self, close other, and acquaintance. Bars denote the group means, and error bars represent 95% Confidence Intervals of the mean

Having said this, the practical recommendations are clear: global health politics should aim at reducing not one but at least two social cognition biases. In the short term, they would take away procedures aimed to reducing fear, anxiety, and depression even but in a long run would prolong life and quality of life (since COVID-19 is extremely dangerous in terms of not only mortality but also in the long-term perspective which we present in the last chapter). Under conditions of real danger, one should be less concerned with well-being and stress reduction and more concerned with protecting human life. There will be time to augment well-being after the grave threat has subsided.

Chapter 3
Time to Worry? Comparative Biases and Health-Related Behaviors in the Time of the COVID-19 Pandemic

The manifestation of unrealistic optimism during the particular period of a pandemic is unquestionably a cognitively interesting phenomenon in its own right. Equally (or perhaps even more) interesting is how cognitive biases are related to the manifestation of specific, e.g., health-promoting, behaviors. After all, you have likely been thinking to yourself for some time: "well, I know what cognitive biases are; I can see that they occur during the COVID-19 pandemic as well. I also remember that they are functional: they enable us to reduce stress, fear, and anxiety. Perhaps, then, this falsehood should not be taken away from us? After all, what's wrong with deluding ourselves about the present and the future?"

These questions are absolutely crucial because the reduction of prolonged stress should have a positive effect on long-term health. Egotistical illusions can therefore be treated as a health-promoting factor.

3.1 Unrealistic Pessimism

Recall at this point that the very idea of our carrying out an extensive program of research on comparative illusions during a pandemic originated in our observation that this distinctive state of vagueness and a sense of widespread danger is very much like the situation in which a radioactive cloud loomed over people's heads in the aftermath of the Chernobyl nuclear power plant accident. At that time, one of the authors of this book and his colleagues (Dolinski et al., 1987) observed the occurrence of unrealistic pessimism. Most of the people in their research felt more vulnerable to radiation exposure than the average person. Of course, in the rather large population studied by these psychologists at the time, there were also those who demonstrated unrealistic optimism. They believed that it would be others, rather than them, who would become ill in the future with diseases that were a consequence of significantly elevated radiation.

W. Kulesza, D. Doliński, *Social Biases During Covid 19*, SpringerBriefs in Psychology, https://doi.org/10.1007/978-3-031-34706-1_3

The aforementioned study also specified the relationship between comparative optimism and pessimism, on the one hand, and the declared intensity of manifestation of various preventive behaviors that could (at least potentially) reduce the effects of radiation, on the other hand. Such behaviors were, for example, drinking Lugol's iodine or refraining from drinking milk (the milkman system was popular in Poland at the time, and fresh unpasteurized milk which came from cows feeding on irradiated grass was delivered to the doors of homes in the morning). Another health-promoting behavior was to refrain from eating fresh vegetables that grew on contaminated soil and to limit time spent outdoors or even keeping windows closed in the home.

It turned out that people exhibiting unrealistic pessimism are far more likely to engage in such behavior than those demonstrating unrealistic optimism. The link between unrealistic optimism and ignoring health recommendations seems quite obvious here: since I think that the disease will affect others rather than me, there is no reason for me to manifest any health-promoting behavior that requires me to make smaller or larger sacrifices. And conversely, the pessimist believes that they are especially vulnerable and declares proactive health-oriented actions. To summarize, optimism seems wildly dangerous for one who falsifies their perception of reality in this way! This then gives rise to the assumption that some social biases are dysfunctional. We should take a closer look at this issue, as it may turn out that in the current (and future!) pandemic, social communication efforts should be aimed not only at encouraging health protection measures (wearing masks, refraining from participating in social gatherings at a time of rising rates of the disease, hand washing, and – above all – vaccination) but also at demolishing people's illusions.

3.2 Unrealistic Optimism: Pre-pandemic Research

The negative association of unrealistic optimism with the manifestation of health-promoting behaviors has also been noted in numerous psychological studies conducted under "normal" conditions, i.e., those in which there was no state of emergency or widespread danger. Moreover, other studies do not rely on the declaration noted in our study in the aftermath of the Chernobyl explosion (pessimistic respondents claimed to actively protect their health, but of course we did not know if they actually did so), so it is possible to see exactly how social biases affect real behavior (health-promoting or health-destroying). For example, it was shown that tobacco smokers who showed unrealistic optimism about getting lung cancer were less likely to quit smoking than those who exhibited no such optimistic bias (Dillard et al., 2006). This means that unrealistic optimists have actively damaged their health by increasing the risk of serious, fatal diseases like lung cancer.

This is not an isolated result: women demonstrating unrealistic optimism about the possibility of developing breast cancer were less likely to undergo mammography screening (McCaul et al., 1996), which directly leads to lower detection of this dangerous type of cancer, reducing the chance of early (and therefore more effective) medical intervention. Another study (Dillard et al., 2009), on the other hand, found that students demonstrating unrealistic optimism about the likelihood of experiencing various problems associated with excessive alcohol consumption actually experienced them more frequently and intensely in the future (this was investigated more than 2 years later). It is worth mentioning in passing that the association of unrealistic optimism with a risky drinking style also occurred in a study conducted by Kim and Niederdeppe (2016). Davidson and Prkachin (1997), in turn, showed that people who were advised to exercise did so less often if they displayed unrealistic optimism about their health status and the potential for it to deteriorate in the future. These researchers also gauged the level of unrealistic optimism in people at risk for coronary heart disease and then invited them to attend a special lecture on preventive health behaviors recommended for such individuals. It turned out that people characterized by unrealistic optimism benefited the least from this lecture (i.e., remembered the least relevant information). Most likely, they decided that there was no point in listening carefully or taking notes because such a threat simply did not apply to them. Summarizing the results of Davidson and Prkachin (1997), we thus see a troubling nexus of detrimental reactions triggered by unrealistic optimism: not only do I actively withdraw from behaviors that are recommended for me, but I fail to acquire new information about my condition, which sets in motion further negative consequences. I will not engage in health-promoting activities because I simply know less about them (than a person unaffected by the tendency to falsify reality). This, in turn, shows how deeply social bias penetrates us: once we are affected by negative changes in our bodies, then, despite reducing anxiety or worry, in the long term, we are bound not only to exacerbate our health problems. And with their onset or aggravation, our rates of psychological discomfort will also increase.

Kim and Niederdeppe (2013), on the other hand, measured participants' levels of unrealistic optimism about infection with the H1N1 virus and asked them about their intention to pay particular attention to hand hygiene (as a proven behavior that protects against infection). It turned out that the relationship between the two phenomena was negative: the more someone exhibited unrealistic optimism, the less they intended to follow medical recommendations.

Treloar and Hopwood (2008), on the other hand, show that unrealistic optimism can lead to either abandoning or delaying help-seeking in conditions where, objectively speaking, the patient needs it (immediately!). Hepatitis C patients believed that the negative side effects of therapy tended to affect other people rather than themselves. When such negative side effects appeared, unrealistically optimistic patients first ignored them for a long time and then reacted with shock and strongly negative affect when confronted with reality. Let us emphasize: hepatitis C is insanely dangerous, and postponing or downplaying treatment directly damages the patient's health! Thus, an exceedingly serious conclusion emerges: unrealistic optimism is a useful short-term psychological mechanism for reducing fear and anxiety but in the long-term a serious detriment when it relates to issues of health. Concluding this review, let us note that a raft of other data on the relationship of unrealistic optimism to the possibility of experiencing various medical conditions and ignoring medical advice is also presented by Perloff (1983), whose work we recommend to the reader interested in the details.

3.3 Unrealistic Optimism in the Midst of the COVID-19 Pandemic

Now we move on to the substance of this work (which is not to say that the previous chapters were superfluous; they constitute a conceptual framework, contextualize our later research, and ultimately produce practical recommendations), that is, to see if and how unrealistic optimism can modify behaviors aimed at protecting one's health. In light of the findings presented so far, it seemed not only to us but also to other researchers very likely that studies of human functioning under conditions of the COVID-19 pandemic would also reveal a negative association of unrealistic optimism with the manifestation (or lack) of health-promoting behavior. This is precisely the very clear negative association between levels of unrealistic optimism and behaviors aimed at protecting one's health that was noted in a large-scale study conducted in four countries (Italy, France, Switzerland, and the United Kingdom) involving more than 12,000 people (McColl et al., 2022). The study took place during the first wave of COVID-19 cases in February and March 2020. They found that levels of unrealistic optimism were negatively correlated with the reported frequency of behaviors such as wearing a mask, avoiding touching one's mouth and nose, using hand sanitizer gel, and avoiding contact with people who look sick. This means that in the case of COVID-19 as well, those who falsify reality are harming themselves! It is also worth mentioning that for other recommended behaviors, such as frequent hand washing, using disposable tissues when sneezing or coughing, and avoiding the use of public transportation, while the association with the level of unrealistic optimism did not reach the conventional level of statistical significance (0.05), it too was negative.

A similar pattern of results was noted by Wise et al. (2020), who conducted their studies in the United States between March 11 and 16, 2020 on a sample of about 1500 people. Their analysis yielded a group of 135 people from this sample who were particularly unlikely to engage in preventive behaviors with respect to the risk of contracting COVID-19 (mainly involving thorough hand washing and limiting the number of direct contacts with other people). It turned out that the effect of unrealistic optimism was particularly strong in this particular group. Juxtaposed with the previous result, therefore, a clear picture is emerging of how in the COVID-19 pandemic unrealistic optimism does harm in the same way as in earlier studies (and discussed in the previous section) on the relationship between social bias and health-oriented behaviors.

Park et al. (2021), in turn, showed that the individuals displaying the strongest unrealistic optimism about the likelihood of contracting COVID-19 also report the least interest in obtaining information from medical and other sources about the disease and how to minimize the likelihood of contracting it. This should not come as a surprise. Since, in their view, it is not they but rather other people who are particularly susceptible to contracting the virus, it is these others, not they, who should seek such information. We note here the consistency with the research cited above on unrealistic optimism and hepatitis C. The results are convergent: not only do we harm ourselves by abandoning health-promoting behaviors when we exhibit cognitive bias in the form of unrealistic optimism, but we also forego access to knowledge that could help us stay healthy!

Oljača et al. (2020), on the other hand, examined people's general tendency to manifest unrealistic optimism (i.e., the belief that various negative events will more likely affect others than oneself) and declared adherence to medical recommendations during a pandemic. It turned out that both measures correlated negatively.

In our research (Izydorczak et al., 2023: https://royalsocietypublishing.org/doi/10.1098/rsos.220775), we decided to go a step further and tested the level of comparative optimism with the declaration of intent to take a vaccine. Note that in the case of COVID-19, vaccination is the cheapest, easiest, and most effective preventive protection to date against death resulting from infection with COVID-19. Thus, examining the relationship between unrealistic optimism and the coronavirus pandemic was also particularly important in that it may facilitate some predictions for human behavior during future pandemics, which would be tackled with newly introduced vaccines.

It is worth stipulating that our study was conducted on data collected from June to August 2020, when COVID-19 vaccines were not yet available (and there was no cause to believe they would soon be ready), so, unable to study the actual act of vaccination, we relied on declarations of willingness to vaccinate. A noteworthy strength of our study was the mini-meta-analysis we conducted (i.e., analyzing the data collected in our various studies and comparing the distribution of results for consistency indicating a stable, strong effect, or inconsistency making it difficult to report a stable phenomenon). We took into account the results of our six studies ($N = 2409$ conducted around the world – Germany, Poland, Italy, etc.). Our participants estimated the risk of contracting COVID-19, so we were able to distinguish three groups of people, which we conventionally called pessimists (who thought they were more at risk than others), realists (the largest group, these people estimated as equal the probability that they themselves would get sick and that another person would get sick), and optimists (those who thought they were less at risk than others).

Figure 3.1 shows the results of our research.

As we can see, the results were surprising. Both pessimists and optimists were more likely than realists to say they would vaccinate whenever possible. The inclination of pessimists to vaccinate is fully understandable and in line with our research conducted after the Chernobyl nuclear power plant explosion: pessimists declared high proactivity toward protecting their health by avoiding exposure to radioactive contamination (avoiding leaving the house, closing windows, not eating contaminated products, and drinking Lugol's iodine). In our research, we may assume that since unrealistic pessimists feel particularly threatened, they are obviously

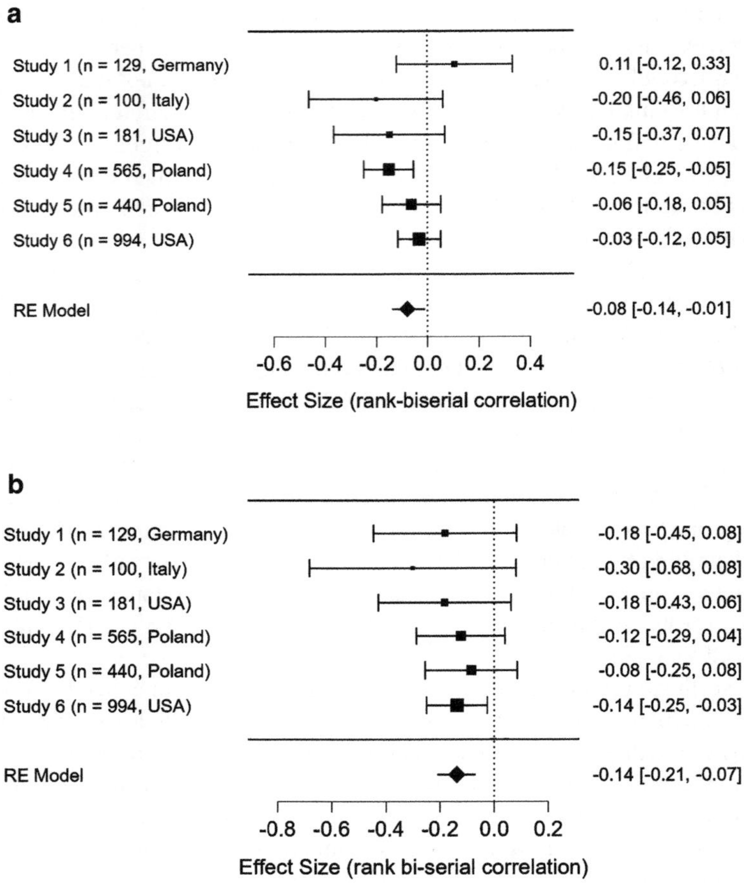

Fig. 3.1 Forest plot (**a**) difference in vaccine intention between comparative realists and comparative optimists, (**b**) difference in vaccine intention between comparative realists and comparative pessimists. (Source: Royal Society Open Science, Copyright: The Royal Society Publishing)

motivated to take measures that reduce this threat, and inoculation is undoubtedly one of them. What is puzzling, however, is the inclination of optimists to be vaccinated and the lack of such propensity among realists. We will begin with the latter issue.

Our third study, conducted in August 2021, a time when vaccines were already available (Izydorczak et al., 2022), sheds some light on explaining why realists declared the weakest willingness to vaccinate. It turned out that realists, in contrast to optimists and pessimists, were less afraid of getting infected with COVID-19 but also more afraid of the vaccine per se. Realists often expressed concern that the vaccines were introduced too hastily, without proper and comprehensive studies.

In this light, however, the positive relationship between unrealistic optimism and declared willingness to vaccinate may seem surprising. However, we believe that this relationship is only superficially illogical. It may surprise us when we treat unrealistic optimism as the independent variable and the tendency to vaccinate as the dependent variable. The belief that I am less likely than the average person to contract a disease should result in a refusal to be vaccinated, rather than a willingness to be vaccinated. However, we should note that the results we obtained only prejudge the correlation relationship, not the direction of a possible (because even this is not certain) causal relationship. So let's try to invert our understanding. Treat the decision to get vaccinated in the near future as the independent variable and the level of unrealistic optimism as the dependent variable. One who has made the decision to get vaccinated against COVID-19 in the near future ("whenever possible") now has a full rational basis for perceiving themself as less vulnerable than the "average other." After all, they know that there are many people in the population who are skeptical of vaccination against COVID-19, so many people will not be vaccinated. With this interpretation, the results regarding optimists cease to be surprising and assume a reasonable logic.

The results of experiments conducted in Brazil (Vieites et al., 2021) seem consistent with such an assumption. The researchers hypothesized that if they focus an individual on the fact that they are demonstrating preventive behaviors, they will consequently reveal higher levels of unrealistic optimism than somebody who is simply asked to estimate the risk of disease for themselves and others. This, we note, is because such an awareness-raising influence increases self-conscientiousness by elevating it, and – as we discussed above – this is heavily associated with social cognition biases. In keeping with this line of reasoning, the researchers have rightly assumed that one of the sources of unrealistic optimism is cognitive egocentrism – the mechanism we outlined in Sect. 1.4, i.e., that one's own behavior is more cognitively accessible to us than other people's behavior. (We simply know perfectly well how we behave and cannot have such equally precise and expansive knowledge of others if only for the reason that we do not see/experience other people's behavior as much as our own.) Through simple interventions, however, it is possible to further increase an individual's cognitive accessibility to information about their appropriate and desirable reactions. In their first experiment, the researchers simply asked people first how often they wore a mask and then estimated their level of unrealistic optimism. In the second study, prior to measuring their degree of unrealistic optimism, participants were asked to determine whether they agreed with the following statement:

> The authorities have recommended mask wearing as a measure to contain the dissemination of the coronavirus. According to experts, wearing a mask when going out significantly reduces the risk of contamination. Do you agree with this statement? ___ Yes ___ No. (Vieites et al., 2021, p. 626)

It turned out that both of these simple interventions led to increased levels of unrealistic optimism. When looking at them, it is essential to consider that the measure of unrealistic optimism was constructed by the researchers in such a way that the lower the bars on the graphs, the higher the level of unrealistic optimism (this refers to the way the authors coded the results; we have already said that there are different methods of measuring and analyzing unrealistic optimism).

3.4 Better than Average

There is also the question of whether the stated intention to vaccinate against COVID-19 will be positively correlated with another positive comparative bias we write about in this book, i.e., the better-than-average effect. In one of our studies (Kulesza et al., 2022b), we decided to test this. The respondents first estimated the extent to which they themselves engage in various behaviors recommended during the pandemic by medical authorities (keeping social distance, wearing masks, frequent hand washing, etc.) and the extent to which the average person of their sex and age does so. This allowed us to calculate a better-than-average effect factor for each participant. We then asked each participant to indicate on an 11-point scale (from "definitely not" to "definitely yes") their intention to take a COVID-19 vaccine as soon as it became available. (We conducted the survey in August 2020, when no such vaccine was available, but it was already rumored to be coming relatively soon.) Regression analysis showed a moderate relationship between the two variables.

Thus, we see that the magnitude of the better-than-average effect is a predictor of intention to vaccinate; but, on the other hand, the relative weakness of this relationship indicates that the tendency to vaccinate is based largely on other mechanisms than the propensity to manifest other health-promoting behaviors. There is no doubt that, from a medical perspective, the most effective way to prevent a pandemic is mass vaccination of the population. From a psychological perspective, however, the situation is quite complex. Indeed, as we have shown in previous sections of this book, cognitive biases may not foster various health-promoting behaviors. The studies we present now, on the other hand, show that they can induce people to get vaccinated.

It is this distinctiveness of vaccination from other forms of protection against infection that may psychologically partly explain why the studies recorded a negative association of the level of unrealistic optimism with the frequency of such medical/health-related behaviors as washing one's hands or limiting real, direct contact with other people but unrealistic optimism was positively associated with the intention to be vaccinated. Perhaps unrealistic optimism is associated differently with behaviors that have already been manifested (or are currently being manifested) and still differently with hypothetical, future behaviors that the individual is only just considering. Whether this is indeed the case could only be conclusively determined by empirical research, which we strongly encourage.

However, it should be emphasized here that the positive relationship declared in our study conducted in Poland (a country with an average vaccination rate) between unrealistic optimism and COVID-19 vaccination did not occur in the study conducted in Romania – a country with a record low level of COVID-19 vaccination and also the highest mortality rate from the disease in Europe (Maftei & Petroi, 2022). Four groups of people were engaged in the study – those declaring they would definitely not vaccinate, those who were hesitant, those declaring they would definitely vaccinate, and those who had already been vaccinated. Unrealistic optimism was examined in relation to both the probability of contracting COVID-19 and the severity of the disease. The respondents were asked to determine the probabilities of both states of affairs for themselves and the average Romanian of their age and sex. It turned out that those declaring that they would definitely not vaccinate exhibited the highest level of unrealistic optimism, the hesitant slightly lower, and those determined to vaccinate the lowest. We should add for the sake of argument that those who had already been vaccinated also reported high optimism (the same as those who definitely did not want to be vaccinated), but in their case, it is difficult to speak of unrealistic optimism. After all, they were comparing themselves with the average person, and the vast majority of the Romanian population was not vaccinated.

As we proceed toward recommendations, summaries, and therefore the conclusions of this book, let us consider the studies presented above in a broader perspective. The McColl et al. (2022) study conducted in four Western European countries and the Maftei and Petroi (2022) study just discussed by us in Romania, as well as the Wise et al. (2020) and Park et al. (2021) studies we mentioned earlier in this book, show clearly that, in certain cases, unrealistic optimism can lead to inappropriate behavior, increasing not only the likelihood of a particular person contracting the disease but consequently the spread of infections and the growth of a pandemic. To put it bluntly, unrealistic optimism thus has destructive consequences both at the individual level (avoidance of health-promoting behaviors) and at the community level (when the mass of people avoids washing their hands thoroughly or wearing masks, a pandemic will develop!). If we additionally consider the fact that, in the realm of health, unrealistic optimism can also prove dangerous for many other diseases and disorders (e.g., Dillard et al., 2006, 2009; McCaul et al., 1996) and the fact that the aforementioned illusion can also be dangerous in areas of human functioning other than health (e.g., Sweeny & Shepperd, 2010; Yang et al., 2007), the question of ways to reduce unrealistic optimism clearly must arise. Moreover, it may turn out that unrealistic optimism in general negatively affects all health-promoting behaviors, significantly degrading the health of the person falsifying reality in this way. In other words, we would like to say that, so far, what has been analyzed is the association of unrealistic optimism with single health-promoting behaviors targeting particular diseases. Probably nobody has yet analyzed the role of unrealistic optimism in downplaying all types of health risks. If it turned to be the case that unrealistic optimism globally influences a particular person's disengagement from a vast number of health-promoting behaviors (e.g., forgoing mammograms, screening and follow-up examinations, excessive alcohol consumption, avoidance of dietary recommendations, etc.), we could speak of a sort of psychological sepsis! Even if this is not the case, the potential (i.e., concerning specific individual risks) harm of unrealistic optimism is beyond question. The vital issue of methods to reduce unrealistic optimism is therefore the focus of the next section of this book.

We also note in passing that in the preceding section we have paid almost no attention to the relationship between the better-than-average illusion and health-promoting behavior. This is because we did not find many works reporting such results. More research is therefore needed, both on the COVID-19 pandemic and the broader aspect of global health. This seems crucial to developing a better understanding (and therefore preparation) for upcoming pandemics (and perhaps other sudden, unpredictable, and massive disasters; we will write more about this in the conclusion of this book).

Chapter 4
Time to Act! Means of Reducing Positive Illusions

You, the reader, are already well aware that in this book we analyze two cognitive positive biases: the better-than-average effect and unrealistic optimism. The former seems to produce negative consequences only when it is acutely amplified, when, to use Baumeister's (1989) language, it ceases to be an illusion and takes the form of a delusion. In such situations, the individual, convinced of their own perfection, may lose motivation to enhance their competence and skills (Brown, 2012; Moore & Healy, 2008). Research also shows that, in certain situations, it can also diminish one's interpersonal attractiveness, especially in the long term (Bonanno et al., 2005). While certainly in some cases the belief that one is better than others can also have – as we have shown above in the context of prevention against COVID-19 – negative consequences for people's functioning in the area of health, by far the second of the biases analyzed in this book, unrealistic optimism, seems more dangerous. In his pioneering article on this positivity bias, Neil Weinstein (1980) already draws attention to the dangers of optimism construed in this way. In doing so, he presents research showing how the magnitude of this positivity bias can be reduced. While we have also discussed a number of works in the broad context of healthcare confirming these preliminary results and presented a detailed analysis of the dangerous link between realistic optimism and the failure to employ active behaviors targeting COVID-19, the key question is "what can be done" to reduce the widespread and dangerous presence of unrealistic optimism during threats such as the coronavirus pandemic.

Recall that the author of the concept of unrealistic optimum, Weinstein, started from the premise that one of the reasons for the occurrence of unrealistic optimism may be a false image of other people. The individual may believe that, for various reasons, they are very likely to be victims of various undesirable events and, on the other hand, lack the competence, motivation, perseverance, or other attributes to achieve desirable states. In other words, while people are aware of their own attributes and competencies, they are not aware that other people also have them. And it is precisely this discrepancy in knowledge about oneself and knowledge about other people, referred to as cognitive egocentrism, that is one of the sources of unrealistic optimism. Now let us look at how cognitive egocentrism is empirically tested for the reduction, or even elimination, of unrealistic optimism.

W. Kulesza, D. Doliński, *Social Biases During Covid 19*, SpringerBriefs in Psychology, https://doi.org/10.1007/978-3-031-34706-1_4

4.1 You Are Not Exceptional, Not at All!

In Weinstein's (1980) pioneering experiment, 120 female students of Rutgers University took part. They were asked to estimate from what percentage of female students at that university they were more likely to experience various negative events and from what percentage of female students they were more likely to have various positive experiences. The respondents were then asked to write down the various factors that lead them to make such judgments. So they were to write down what actually makes them more likely than others to have positive things happen in their lives and what makes them relatively (i.e., compared to other people) less likely to experience various traumatic events. After doing so, they were handed a folder with pages that had been written by five other female participants who had been surveyed earlier in the experiment. They were asked to read these notes carefully. By this procedure, the students were able to see that other people gave a whole host of different reasons why they would be highly likely to experience desirable states and avoid undesirable ones. Finally, respondents again filled out a questionnaire allowing them to estimate their level of unrealistic optimism. It turned out that this procedure led to a significant decrease in the level of bias analyzed here.

In subsequent studies, Weinstein (1983) used a slightly different procedure, although the idea of reducing unrealistic optimism itself remained the same. This time, both men and women were studied, and participants were randomly assigned to one of three experimental conditions. In the first condition (control), they simply estimated their chances of experiencing various negative states of affairs, comparing them to the chances of the average university student of their own sex. In the second condition (own risk), the participants were asked to think about whether, in their case, the possibility of avoiding undesirable events might be influenced by the various factors presented to them, and only then did they measure their level of unrealistic optimism about various negative events. In the third group (information), participants were shown the same list of factors, but at the same time, with each question they were told what percentage of previously surveyed students at that university considered the factor to be important in their own case. The reduction or increase in the level of unrealistic optimism can be described in this experiment by comparing the estimates made by participants in the last two groups with those made by participants in the control condition, that is, those who were simply asked to provide risk assessments.

Weinstein asked participants to estimate their own chances of avoiding negative events compared to those of the average student for ten different events. He chose five for which very strong unrealistic optimism had been recorded in earlier studies (diabetes, heart attack, drinking problem, suicide, lung cancer) and five for which unrealistic optimism was weak or not reported at all (other form of cancer, ulcer, tooth decay, high blood pressure, auto accident injury, mugging).

It turned out that among the participants subjected to the "information" type of intervention (reduction of cognitive egocentrism, orientation to others), there was a marked reduction in the level of unrealistic optimism with regard to events where the research usually recorded high levels of this bias, and except for one case (auto accident injury), there was no change in their belief about the chances of avoiding undesirable conditions with regard to events where the bias was generally weak. In contrast, there was an increase in the level of unrealistic optimism among participants who reflected only on their own situation (own risk group, where self-centeredness boosts egocentrism). Interestingly, this effect appeared both for events in which unrealistic optimism is usually noted and for events in which it usually does not appear or is weak.

We can therefore see that one way to reduce unrealistic optimism may be to make people aware that they are not unique with regard to certain events – other people also have various attributes or competencies that may, in their individual case, favor the avoidance of undesirable states. This assumption is consonant with the findings of Weinstein and Lachendro's (1982) experiment, in which it was shown that even just getting people to think about various factors that can reduce the risk of others experiencing negative events may to some degree reduce the level of positive illusion discussed here.

A number of years later, Rothman et al. (1996) took a more systematic look at this regularity. They had reliable statistics at their disposal on the probability of various negative states of affairs for the American population. Thus, for example, the probability of at least one divorce in a lifetime was 38% at the time the experiment was conducted, for pneumonia ending in death 2.2% for women and 1.9% for men, and for alcohol dependence or problems resulting from excessive drinking 4.5% for women and as high as 19.5% for men.

The experiment reported here involved female students who were randomly divided into three groups. In the first group, real statistics were presented on the probabilities of various negative events occurring in an American woman's life (such as divorce, alcoholism, chlamydia, depression requiring treatment, or reaching a weight 20% above the norm). In the second group, these statistics were fabricated by giving the participants twice the actual values. In the third group, the respondents were also given false data, but the figures were 150% of the actual values. They were asked to indicate the probabilities that various negative states of affairs would happen to them.

The results were unequivocal. When the respondents were presented with real statistics, they exhibited unrealistic optimism. This illusion was amplified when they were given fabricated statistics suggesting that the risk to the population was lower than it actually was. If, on the other hand, they were provided with false statistics that overstated the risk, they also made higher estimates of the probability that negative events might be their lot. Note, however, that while this is clear evidence that, in estimating risks to themselves, people take into account the probability that such an event could befall the average person in their population, this does not necessarily lead directly to the phenomenon of unrealistic optimism. In other words, the question is whether people demonstrate a belief that they are less likely to experience various negative states of affairs from the statistical values they are provided.

It turned out that in circumstances when they were given falsified statistics suggesting that the risk was higher than it actually was, this was the case. Under such conditions, the women in the study believed that they were clearly less likely to experience such events than the average American woman. However, if the participants were given statistics falsely suggesting that the probability of experiencing various negative events was lower than the actual probability, not only did they not manifest unrealistic optimism but actually considered themselves slightly more likely to experience undesirable conditions than the average American woman. In summary, there is a very interesting interrelation here. If we mislead someone by suggesting that the objective (statistical) probability of some negative event occurring in the life of a person from the group to which they belong is lower than it really is, then, while they will incorrectly assume that the probability of them experiencing it is low (i.e., they will think it is lower than objective statistics suggest), they will not, at the same time, manifest unrealistic optimism. They will not believe that they are less vulnerable than most other people (and may even believe that they are slightly more vulnerable than they are). If, on the other hand, we present them with falsified statistics, from which it will appear that the threat, statistically speaking, is high (more accurately, higher than it would appear from objective data), then they will overestimate the threat to themselves, while at the same time demonstrating heightened unrealistic optimism. Thus, we can conclude that misleading people about such statistics is a double-edged sword and therefore counterproductive. We also cannot overlook the ethical aspect here. After all, lying to patients or clients of a doctor or psychotherapist must not be condoned. Thus, although the experiment presented here, aimed at identifying the mechanism responsible for reducing unrealistic optimism, is cognitively meritorious, we cannot recommend the described interaction as a way of reducing this bias.

4.2 Don't Look Away: Think About the Danger!

You may recall that unrealistic optimism helps reduce fear and anxiety. Thus, it can be assumed that it allows us to disregard that which threatens us. Anxiety, after all, concentrates our attention on the factor that causes it. So let us look at another possibility, consistent with this assumption, for reducing such positive illusions, which comes from research published by Frank McKenna and Ian Albery (2001).

In contrast to the researchers whose experiments we have discussed above (where the effect of reducing egocentrism on lowering unrealistic optimism was tested), McKenna and Albery assumed that a decrease in unrealistic optimism could be achieved by directing one's attention to oneself, rather than to other people. However, this is not a matter of focusing on various real or hypothetical competencies or mental dispositions that can help a person avoid a threat but on the negative event itself as such. A situation in which the individual can imagine being a participant in, or actually a victim of, such accidents can increase their subjective belief that this is possible (it is difficult to fear something we don't know about and don't pay attention to, such as Ebola for Europeans). In turn, this is easiest to imagine if one has already experienced such a situation.

McKenna and Albery (2001) explored this possibility in a simple fashion and ensured that their study included drivers with a variety of driving experiences: those who, according to police records, had never been in an accident, those who had caused a minor accident that did not injure its participants, those who had caused a serious accident in which someone else was injured, and those who had caused an equally serious accident in which they themselves were victims. Participants were asked to estimate how skilled they were at driving compared to the average driver and how safe they drive, as well as how likely they were (also, of course, compared to the average driver) to cause a traffic accident in the future. Thus, we see that we are dealing here with both questions pertaining to the realm of better than average (the first two questions) and to that of unrealistic optimism (question three).

It turned out that, with regard to the first two questions, two groups proved distinct from the other two. Common sense would dictate that drivers who had never caused an accident considered themselves more skilled and safer drivers than those in the other groups. After all, it is difficult to assume that one is an unsafe driver if one has never caused an accident. Drivers who themselves suffered in an accident they caused considered themselves, in turn, to be the least capable and the least safe of the four groups surveyed. This, too, is perfectly understandable: having accidents = not driving safely.

However, it turned out that when estimating the likelihood of causing an accident in the future, no differences were noted between the four groups of drivers. For the sake of clarity, we should add that strong unrealistic optimism was recorded in all four groups. Thus, summarizing these results, it can be said that personal experiences can change unrealistic beliefs about one's own above-average abilities but do not reduce the level of unrealistic optimism and perception of the future. This may yield serious lessons for pandemic management and the feeling of unrealistic optimism: regardless of whether we have been affected by the virus, we unrealistically assume that it will not affect us (anymore), but it will affect others!

As part of our own empirical research program on the positive illusions experienced by people during a pandemic, we also faced failure in developing a technique to reduce the level of unrealistic optimism. Our idea was inspired by the so-called cognitive accessibility heuristic (Tversky & Kahneman, 1973). A good example of this phenomenon is a study whose participants read a list of names. In one case, it consisted of the names of 19 famous men and 20 rather unknown women, and in the other case, it consisted of the names of 19 famous women and 20 little-known men. When the participants were then asked whether there were more women or men on the list, those reading the first list mistakenly thought there were more men, while those reading the second list thought there were more women. The explanation for these mistakes is that familiar names were cognitively easier to remember and recall (because they were familiar) when it came to answering the question of whether men or women dominated the list in terms of numbers.

Building on the concept of the accessibility heuristic, Norbert Schwarz and colleagues concluded that in certain situations, people can base inferences about their own characteristics on the extent to which certain information is accessible to their cognitive processes (Schwarz et al., 1991). Some participants in the experiment were asked to recall 6 episodes from their own lives when they behaved assertively, while others were asked to recall 12 such episodes. Subsequently, they completed a self-assessment and were asked to evaluate, among other things, their own assertiveness (understood as a personality trait).

It turned out that those who were previously tasked with recalling 6 episodes were considered more assertive than those who recalled 12 such events. Why? Recalling six episodes of one's own assertive behavior is quite easy, and probably each of us can perform this task. By then answering the question "how assertive are you?," the participants have a solid basis for thinking of themselves as people endowed with such a trait: "Since I can easily recall situations in which I reacted assertively, it means that I am assertive." However, recalling 12 such episodes is difficult or even very difficult for most people (for us, the authors of this book, it is very difficult). Thus, if the participants of the study are asked how assertive they are, their inference proceeds as follows: "Since I had so much difficulty recalling real situations from my own life in which I reacted assertively, it means that I'm probably not very assertive."

Seeking to apply the above results to the pandemic context, we hypothesized that the same might be true of unrealistic optimism and the assumption that one is less likely to contract COVID-19 than other, similar people (we discussed this research in Sect. 3.3). In designing our study, we assumed that if we asked people to give a small number of reasons for believing that they were less likely to experience a negative event (contracting COVID-19) than the average person, it would be an easy task for them. However, if we ask them to give a large number of such reasons, the task becomes difficult. Consequently, in the first of these cases, people should demonstrate heightened unrealistic optimism ("My risk of contracting COVID-19 is lower than that of other, similar people"), but in the second, the degree of this positive illusion should decrease ("it's hard for me to give reasons why I'm actually at less risk so I suppose I'm in the same danger as other, similar people").

In our experiment (Kulesza et al., 2023c), we conducted an online survey of a large group of subscribers to an online university portal for the dissemination of scientific knowledge. We randomly divided the participants into four groups. In the first (control) group, they simply estimated the probability that they themselves would become ill with COVID-19 and estimated the probability that an average subscriber of that portal of their sex would become ill. In the other groups, before making such an estimate, they were asked to list (3, 6, or 9, respectively) factors that should prevent them from becoming ill with COVID-19 themselves, and only after doing so did they answer the same two questions we asked in the control condition.

While we had presumed that an individual's generating six and certainly nine reasons why they were at low risk of getting sick would diminish their unrealistic optimism, nothing of the sort occurred. In addition, we found that the more reasons people gave for remaining healthy in a pandemic, the higher their level of unrealistic optimism was.

So, as we can see, we failed to confirm our assumptions. Perhaps this was because generating even nine reasons to justify one's own optimism was not difficult enough for our participants. (Unfortunately, we did not control for this in our experiment.) It is also possible that our proposed method of reducing unrealistic optimism, while ineffective for contracting a virus during a pandemic, would be effective in other situations. Only future research can answer these questions.

Further research is also undoubtedly needed on the suggestion for reducing unrealistic optimism presented by Hye Kyung Kim and Jeff Niederdeppe (2016). They addressed the problem of risky drinking by college students. They noted that "dry" information about the harms of alcohol and behaviors that can lead to alcoholism or other problems associated with excessive drinking is not very impressive to students, who prefer to party hard with huge amounts of beer or whiskey. They also noted that the level of unrealistic optimism they measured in the student population is clearly related to such alcohol-fueled, leisure activities presenting health risks.

How did the study work? The unrealistic optimists were provided with either dry descriptions saying that drinking large amounts of alcohol was very harmful, or they were introduced to narratives from a student who related that heavy partying based mainly on getting drunk had led him to considerable health problems and an inability to concentrate on his studies (e.g., increasing difficulty in completing homework assignments) during the experiment. The hard-partying student also added that he by no means realized that drinking alcohol could lead to such a predicament. In the control conditions of this experiment, the students were not given any information about the consequences of alcohol use or abuse. All of the participants were asked, in turn, what they thought the likelihood was that they themselves would experience negative consequences of alcohol use during the current semester.

It turned out – contrary to the expectations of the study's authors – that the aforementioned perceived threat was the same in all three experimental conditions (i.e., the "dry" information, narrative, and control conditions). Note, however, that Kim and Niederdeppe examined the level of unrealistic optimism only at the beginning of their study, and after the experimental manipulation, they asked the participants only about the threat they perceived in relation to themselves. The lack of measurement of an analogous threat to the "average other," therefore, makes it impossible to judge whether the narratives bear any relation to unrealistic optimism per se. This issue therefore requires further empirical exploration, as we have already noted.

4.3 Chameleon? Failed!

As part of our research program, we considered whether, for example, doctors – when visiting and talking to patients – or others directly interacting for health purposes with people affected by the COVID-19 pandemic should employ the common method of mimicry, an imitation also called the "chameleon effect" in the literature. There were several justifications for choosing this technique to change views of comparative biases. First, mimicry has been shown to reduce egocentrism: a mechanism we discussed in the first chapter that is a key factor in the constitution of comparative biases. In numerous studies it was shown that mimicry changes the social focus from "me" toward "others" (Lakin et al., 2008; Van Baaren et al., 2004) and changes in social orientation from "me" to "you" create greater tendency to perform mimicry (Castelli et al., 2009; Leighton et al., 2010; Van Swol & Drury-Grogan, 2017).

Participants of our experiment (Kulesza et al., 2022a) for 10 min interacted online with the confederate. The study took place under strict lockdown, so exposure to the COVID-19 threat was imminent, making this experiment especially relevant: participants were not asked to "imagine" being in a pandemic (see also Dolinski, 2018). To stress the focus of the ongoing coronavirus pandemic, the topic of the interview concerned opinions on the ongoing COVID-19 pandemic. In the mimicry condition, the confederate repeated some verbal statements expressed by participant, while in the control condition the confederate only assessed understanding of the statements ("yes," "I understand"; see details for this manipulation, Kulesza et al., 2014).

Contrary to our expectations – backfired – it fueled the unrealistic optimism bias in estimation of risk of COVID-19 infection. Importantly, it is probably the first experiment in the body of research on comparative biases showing that a specific manipulation may fuel this phenomena, indicating that future studies should also research this area.

Our next empirical program, on the possibility of using mass media for this purpose, turned out to be more conclusive in terms of finding a way to reduce levels of unrealistic optimism (Dolinski et al., 2022).

4.4 Media Intervention Program

As we already know, the mechanism of cognitive egocentrism leads the individual to focus on their own behavior, while being less aware of other people's actions. This makes them think they have a better chance than others to avoid various negative events. Part of the techniques described above for lowering the intensity of unrealistic optimism are thus focused on making one realize that other people also take various actions that are motivated by their desire to reduce risk (Weinstein, 1980, 1983; Weinstein & Lachendro, 1982; Rothman et al., 1996). Note, however, when people estimate the risk of contracting an easily spread virus during a pandemic, the situation is much more complex than with regard to diseases and disorders such as alcoholism or obesity. In cases of alcoholism or the possibility of obesity, the actions and behaviors of others have a very limited impact on the individual's situation. One may or may not become an alcoholic and may or may not become obese regardless of what other people (especially those outside their circle of acquaintances) do.

In the case of infectious diseases, however, the situation is quite different. The behavior of other people who can transmit viruses remains in close relation to the situation of the individual, who, willingly or unwillingly, must come into contact with such people, at least from time to time. This creates, from the perspective of factors that can affect the level of unrealistic optimism, a unique situation. On the one hand, making the individual aware that others also frequently wash their hands, keep physical distance, disinfect surfaces in the places they are in, or wear masks should make us realize that we are not unique in these respects and, consequently, reduce our level of unrealistic optimism. On the other hand, however, the conviction that many others are acting unwisely and not following medical advice should make us realize that this increases the likelihood that we ourselves will get infected (from such people) and become ill. Nevertheless, in the case of the COVID-19 pandemic, many of us have contracted this dangerous disease at least once, and certainly we all know people affected by the virus. Moreover, unfortunately, some of us have suffered the death of a loved one from COVID-19. Consequently, influenced by just such information, we should also experience a reduction in unrealistic optimism.

In doing so, we should note that during a pandemic the mass media can present all sorts of images and information about people's behavior. They can – and do! – both create the impression that the vast majority of the population follows medical recommendations and publicize cases indicating that there are numerous situations in which people do not wear masks or ignore bans on mass events (such as rock concerts). As part of our empirical research program, we decided to test how the aforementioned information of various kinds (other people follow medical recommendations vs. other people don't follow them) affects the level of unrealistic optimism that individuals demonstrate.

Our first study included 350 participants of both sexes randomly assigned to one of three experimental conditions (Dolinski et al., 2022). (The initial pool had 360 participants, but it turned out that 10 of them were infected with COVID-19, so they were excluded from analysis.) For the two experimental groups, the participants read newspaper articles we had prepared especially for them. In the first condition, they made clear that people were widely ignoring medical advice on how to function in a coronavirus pandemic. In the second condition, the thrust of the articles was completely different. They indicated that people were universally following medical guidelines. Participants in the third group (control conditions) did not read any of the newspaper articles we had prepared. They were asked questions about their own risk of getting infected and that of the "average other" (a classic measure of unrealistic optimism). We present the results of this experiment in Fig. 4.1.

As we can see, the pattern of results for respondents who read articles about people ignoring medical recommendations is the same as in the control condition. In both cases, people demonstrate unrealistic optimism, and estimates of risk to self and risk to the average other are also almost identical. However, the situation is different when people have read information about others behaving responsibly, and public compliance with medical recommendations is widespread. This time the unrealistic optimism vanished! For the sake of clarity, we add that this effect was achieved because people began to perceive themselves as more likely to get sick. The effect is therefore analogous to that obtained in earlier studies dealing with

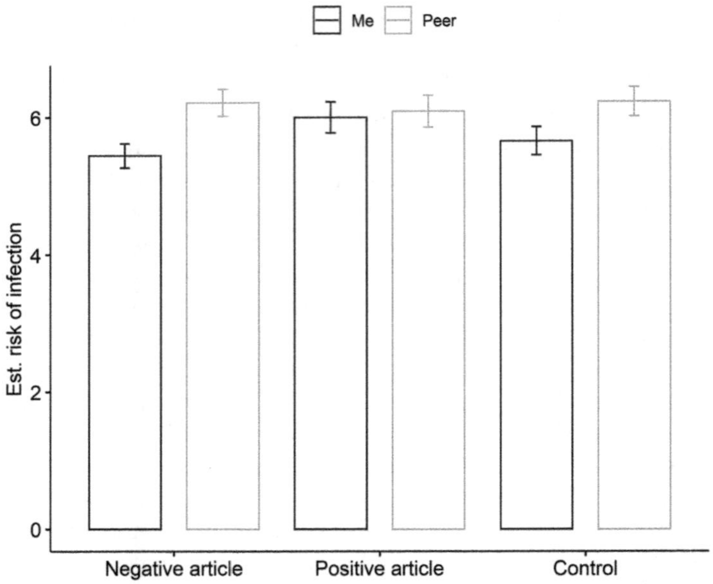

Fig. 4.1 Unrealistic optimism effect in three experimental conditions
Source: *Applied Psychology: Health and Well-Being, 14*, p. 505
Copyright: Wiley
Note: Bars represent mean values, error bars represent standard error of mean

noncommunicable diseases and other adverse conditions (Weinstein, 1980, 1983; Weinstein & Lachendro, 1982; Rothman et al., 1996).

In our second study, we decided to see if this pattern of results would be replicated in conditions using media that employ images rather than words. This time, we presented 600 participants with videos (no words, conversations, or commentary were heard) showing the behavior of a group of people in a coffee shop. Some people saw a video in which people ignored medical recommendations (they did not disinfect their hands when entering the café despite passing a visible dispenser; they did not wear face masks; they crowded in line at the counter when choosing pastries and ordering coffee), while some were shown a video in which people behaved completely differently – they complied fully with all medical recommendations. Participants were not shown any video in the control condition.

Analysis of the results of this experiment quite unexpectedly revealed an entirely different structure to those of the experiment discussed previously. As we will see in Fig. 4.2, people observing others who behave as prescribed medically felt less at risk overall, that is, they exhibited unrealistic optimism. Compared to participants in the control condition, they believed that both they themselves and the "average other" were at less risk. At the same time, these participants demonstrated the same strong unrealistic optimism as those in the control condition. It was the "average other" who, in their view, was more likely to contract COVID-19. In contrast, we noted a decrease in unrealistic optimism among the participants who had watched the video showing people ignoring medical recommendations.

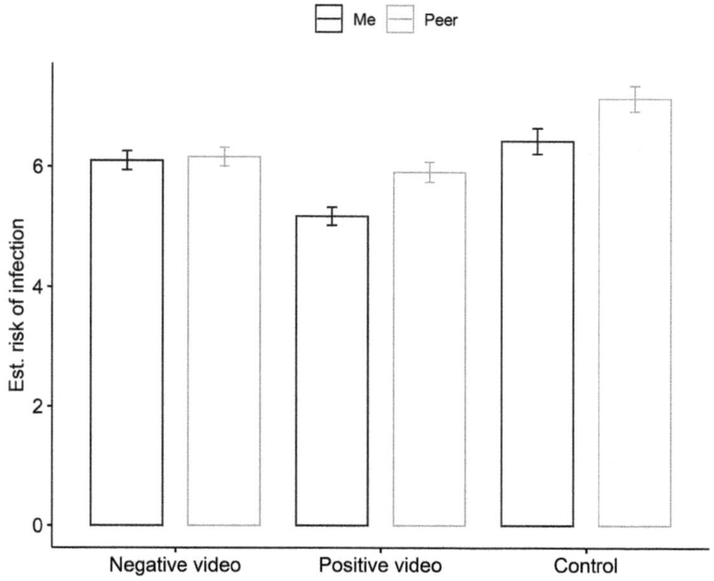

Fig. 4.2 Unrealistic optimism effect in positive and negative movie conditions
Source: *Applied Psychology: Health and Well-Being, 14*, p. 508
Copyright: Wiley
Note: Bars represent mean values, error bars represent standard error of mean

Thus, we see that a completely different pattern of results was obtained when the participants read texts versus when they viewed images. In the first case (reading a newspaper piece), unrealistic optimism was reduced under conditions when the participants learned that other people were behaving properly and following medical recommendations, while in the second case (observing other people's behavior in a video), the pattern was exactly the opposite – it happened only when people saw others completely ignoring medical recommendations.

How can these discrepancies be explained? We assumed that the pivotal factor is that reading articles is more effortful than watching videos, as reflected in the results of numerous studies (e.g., Dalrymple & Scheufele, 2007; Eveland et al., 2002). Thus, reading an article reduces cognitive egocentrism and prompts us to focus on the threat and assume that, because other people exhibit different health-promoting behaviors, there is no reason for us to continue believing that we are less likely than they to get sick. Watching a video, which is less effortful because it is less demanding, is not as likely to induce analytical thinking. In conditions where the participant sees people ignoring recommendations, the image acts as a danger signal: "because of people like them, I can get sick." In other words, the key to explaining the different patterns of results in our two aforementioned experiments is found in the fact that particular forms of media lead people to process the information they receive more or less carefully.

The results of our third experiment, in which we independently manipulated the form of the message (written text vs. video footage) and information about other people's behavior (consistent with medical recommendations vs. inconsistent with them) essentially confirmed the validity of this interpretation.

4.5 Teach and Learn?

In the first chapter of this book, we have already presented one of our studies conducted at the very beginning of the pandemic (Study #2; Kulesza et al., 2021). As a reminder, unrealistic optimism was found in three different countries, Poland, Kazakhstan, and Iran, and this comparative bias did not disappear. In that paper, we also reported a second study that may indicate some directions for another mechanism responsible for reducing unrealistic optimism, i.e., knowledge and education.

This survey was conducted in the Polish highest tertiary referral pediatric hospital with almost 1000 beds, up to 50,000 hospitalizations, and about 120,000 ambulatory clinic visits per year and thus in a frontline hospital not only in terms of fighting COVID-19 pandemic but in the volume and complexity of cases. We were interested if healthcare professionals would present unrealistic optimism or not, since both scenarios were possible: (1) to the best of our knowledge, so far there is no research showing that some work environments are free from unrealistic bias; thus we could expect that healthcare professionals would report this comparative bias as well; (2) since healthcare professionals are not only highly educated in terms of academic knowledge but first and foremost during COVID-19 pandemic were witnesses – to an extent inaccessible for the average person – to the severity of this virus, as a result, they would not report this bias. In this case, formal education and/or exposure to the severity of the pandemic both would "educate."

More than 200 healthcare professionals (doctors/physicians, nurses, first responders/paramedics) completed the survey. Importantly, they did so during the first wave of the COVID-19 pandemic, when we assessed unrealistic optimism in Poland. They delivered surprising results: no unrealistic optimism was found! A summary of the results can be found in Tables 4.1 and 4.2.

A very cautious practical conclusion is that we should educate (in the formal sense; academically, through coursework; "in real life," by showcasing the effects of the pandemic). We note that this professional group possesses both qualities. While

Table 4.1 Summary of the results from the second study (dependent samples t-test)

	Unrealistic optimism bias						
	Myself		Coworker				
Sample	*M*	*SD*	*M*	*SD*	*t*	*p*	*d*
Whole sample	5.96	1.73	5.87	1.7	1.06	.290	.07
Doctors	5.94	2.11	5.87	2.03	.66	.511	.07
Nurses	5.99	1.45	5.88	1.46	.91	.363	.09

Table 4.2 Summary of the results from the second study (independent samples t-test)

	Work area						
	Nurses		Doctors				
Unrealistic optimism bias	*M*	*SD*	*M*	*SD*	*t*	*p*	*d*
Myself	5.99	1.45	5.94	2.11	.19	.849	.03
Coworker	5.88	1.46	5.87	2.03	.04	.970	.01

formulating the above cautious recommendation, we would like at the same time to strongly emphasize several caveats. The referenced study may suggest the previously described relationship between exposure to COVID-19 (direct, contact with patients, and indirect, knowledge of the disease), but it must be kept in mind that this was not a classic experiment! Therefore, it is possible that other factors specific to this professional group (e.g., the extreme fatigue experienced during this period) prevented it from exhibiting egotistical illusions.

In concluding this chapter, we would like to note that the search for methods to reduce unrealistic optimism is, without a doubt, of great importance in developing recommendations both for therapists conducting individual work with overly optimistic clients and for policy-makers implementing mass media information policies in the face of all sorts of crises. Our review of this subject shows that while psychologists have succeeded in making some empirical findings, further intensive research on this important problem is imperative. This is important because the effects of COVID-19 are multifaceted and long term. It would often seem that if we have "survived" COVID-19, then the worst is behind us. It turns out that there are many more long-term effects, which, from the perspective of this book, broadens the horizon of the sense of struggle to ensure that as many people as possible do not get sick in the future. We will discuss this in the next chapter.

Chapter 5
Time to Bother! Longitudinal Impact of the COVID-19 Pandemic (and Others Too): Why Dismantling Social Cognition Biases Is Absolutely Crucial to Save Not Only Lives

As we close this volume, we must ask ourselves: perhaps there is no reason to raise the alarm? COVID-19 used to dominate the headlines, but now it's virtually absent. Maybe there is nothing to be afraid of? "Those who are supposed to die will die, but the rest of the sick will get sick and then be fine," some of us seem to be saying. Should we relax and accept that this book is historical, rather than one constructing scenarios for the future? In our opinion, it is very much a book about the future. In this chapter, we briefly review the effects of COVID-19, not in terms of mortality but rather of the impact the coronavirus has had and will continue to have on us. Why are we doing this? To illustrate the long-term effects and encourage better prevention in advance of future pandemics. There really is "something worth fighting for."

The ongoing COVID-19 pandemic has reminded us of a truth that we have either actively repressed or simply forgotten: pandemics entail a massive serving of – often existential – anxiety for us and our loved ones, anxiety for our health and our future, in economic terms as well as psychological: well-being, stress, burnout, and depression. Thus, it is clear that the global threat to life and health resulting from the emergence of pandemics engenders a difficult-to-overestimate and analogous threat to our psychological and psychiatric well-being.

The paradox of the current threat is that, despite our own experience, we act as if we have none. On the one hand, an analogous pandemic took place more than a century ago (the so-called Spanish flu), and essentially – owing to censorship that shielded the public fear of the victims of World War I – it did not penetrate broadly into the consciousness of those living at the time, while reducing the risk of massive psychological and psychiatric effects caused by this fear. Only historians (of pandemics, of medicine) uncovered this danger by describing – in retrospect – the terrible toll it took. On the other hand, the less indiscriminate polio pandemic left its mark on those living roughly 50–70 years ago (and thus a small group of the readers of these words). We remember it faintly (if we were alive in those days, e.g., Dariusz Dolinski) or not at all (if we had not yet come into being, e.g., Wojciech Kulesza). Eyewitnesses to this tragedy (our parents, grandparents) who went through this

W. Kulesza, D. Doliński, *Social Biases During Covid 19*, SpringerBriefs in Psychology, https://doi.org/10.1007/978-3-031-34706-1_5

tragedy in full consciousness are no longer alive or are nearing the end of their lives, so the experience of the psychological and psychiatric consequences does not have a place in our collective consciousness.

As a consequence of both these factors, analyses of the psychological results of pandemics are rather historical, with the present times visiting the first (and painful) lesson on a living social organism: ourselves. The current pandemic is creating a collective consciousness of mainly the medical effects just mentioned, without yet heeding the psychological and psychiatric effects. Before summarizing the discussed methods of self-deception for coping with the unpredictable future, anxiety, and stress resulting from the COVID-19 pandemic, we offer a momentary reflection on what psychological effects – both short and long term – the pandemic brings.

We will begin with the short-term ones, which are not only more intuitive (they are experienced directly by us and our loved ones; there is already a rich literature describing this time horizon) but, for obvious reasons, are better understood than the long-term ones. There is not yet enough research on the long-term effects of the ongoing COVID-19 pandemic, as the primary factor in solidifying knowledge from research findings is passage of the necessary time. For this reason, the following section references reasonably up-to-date knowledge as of the fall of 2022 (so only 2 and a half years after the COVID-19 pandemic was announced).

5.1 Psychological and Psychiatric Consequences

It probably will not come as a surprise that the COVID-19 pandemic was associated with an increase in anxiety and depression (Huang & Zhao, 2020; Prati, 2021; Prati & Mancini, 2021; Taylor et al., 2020; Vanderlind et al., 2021). What seems less clear, however, is the dynamics of these processes during the pandemic. This issue was the focus of a study by Debowska et al. (2022). More than 7000 Polish students were surveyed with various questionnaires during five phases of the pandemic: (1) March 1–15, 2020, i.e., immediately after the first cases of COVID-19 were identified in Poland; (2) March 16–22, after the first restrictions were introduced, e.g., closure of schools and universities, cancellation of mass events; (3) March 23–29, when regulations were introduced restricting direct human contact; (4) March 30–April 5, when a ban on entering forests and parks was introduced and it was established that people should not approach each other at a distance of less than 2 m; (5) April 6–30, when some restrictions were lifted but a mandate to cover mouths and noses was introduced. In addition to tools measuring anxiety and depression, they also examined levels of perceived stress and suicidal tendencies. As we can see in Fig. 5.1, the level of emotional dysfunction not only depended on the period in which the study was conducted but also on the sex of the subjects.

Another psychological disorder often reported following the COVID-19 pandemic is post-traumatic stress disorder (PTSD – Mak et al., 2009; Mazza et al., 2020; Parker et al., 2015), noted in almost one-third of COVID-19 survivors (Cai et al., 2020; Mazza et al., 2020). Chinese studies show that the mere information of

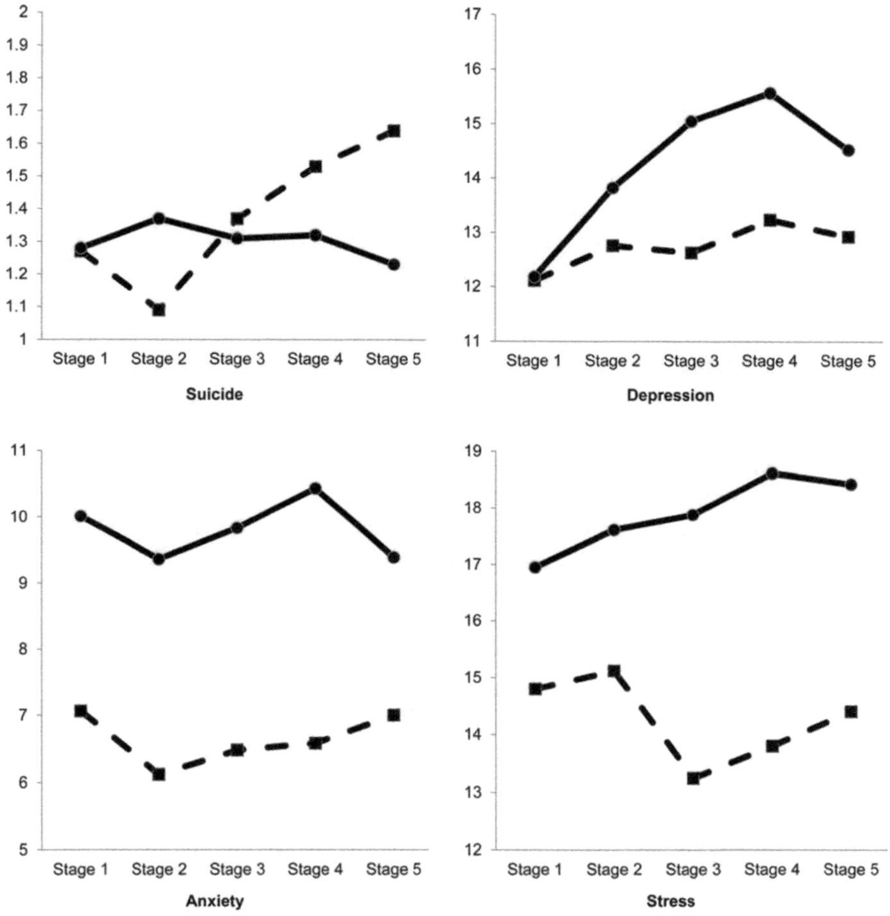

Fig. 5.1 University students' stress, depression, anxiety, and suicidality in the early stages of the COVID-19 pandemic
Source: *Psychological Medicine, 52*, p. 3746
Copyright: Cambridge University Press
Notes: Solid line = females; dashed line = males

a positive test result can trigger PTSD (Yuan et al., 2021), leading to the conclusion that it is not only the disease that produces psychological effects but also the mere fact of being diagnosed with it. The question may arise as to where the aforementioned consequences of infection come from. The answer may be provided by studies showing that the effect of the ongoing pandemic (affecting healthy people as well) is social isolation, which subsequently leads not only to the depression just mentioned (Clair et al., 2021) but to other disorders as well. Studies of the etiology of post-traumatic stress disorder commonly draw attention to the role of lack of social support (e.g., Gros et al., 2016). Limiting direct social contact, on the one hand, and people's anxiety-driven focus on themselves, on the other, clearly promoted the development of PTSD.

Finally, it turns out that the pandemic makes its mark on us by not only infecting us per se but by exacerbating existing diseases or mental disorders. It has been shown, for example, that the aforementioned isolation (arising from the quarantine) caused people who had completed treatment for OCD prior to the pandemic to report an increase in hand-washing compulsions during the quarantine as a result of campaigns mandating frequent disinfection to prevent transmission of the virus (Davide et al., 2020; Kumar & Somani, 2020).

One community particularly affected by the COVID-19 pandemic and its psychological and psychiatric consequences is the school environment of students and teachers, starting from early childhood education. It has been shown, for example, that young children not only fear infection with the virus but also fear further transmission of COVID-19 to the elderly, who, as children know, should be especially protected (Idoiaga et al., 2020). In turn, older children (and teachers) have been noted – as a result of the COVID-19 pandemic – to experience increased fear and stress (Browning et al., 2021; USAID, 2021). In academia as well, a decline in various mental health indicators has been reported (Savage et al., 2020), indicating, for example, an increase in suicidal thoughts and depression (Wang et al., 2020).

Against the background of psychological effects in the school environment, we turn to consideration of the long-term effects of the ongoing pandemic. The group of outcomes discussed below is not only less intuitive (it is difficult to predict the long-term effects of something that is currently afflicting us), but for obvious reasons, research on this topic is still scarce.

5.2 COVID-19 Pandemic = School Closures = Longitudinal Social Disaster

In January 2022, the World Bank, Global Education Evidence Advisory Panel, UK Foreign, Commonwealth and Development Office (FCDO), and UNICEF Office of Research-Innocenti published an analysis titled "Prioritizing Learning During COVID-19: The Most Effective Ways to Keep Children Learning During and Post-Pandemic," which captures the essence of the long-term psychological losses: children and adolescents were hardest hit by the pandemic. Pupils lost access to education and related services. The analysis was based on a broader perspective than the experience of people in Western Europe, developed Asian countries like South Korea and Japan, or North America. The report takes into account losses for underdeveloped or developing countries, the regions of the world that, after all, have the highest concentration per capita of the world's children. In these countries, schools were either closed for longer periods during rising illness rates or did not open at all for months or even years. Children in these areas of the world did not have the opportunity for distance learning most often because teachers did not have access to computers either. Demonstrating the scale of long-term losses, it is sufficient to mention that the report indicates that the ongoing COVID-19 pandemic affected 1.6 billion children, who were kept out of school because of it.

Even at this early stage in the analysis of the report (and this chapter), the question may arise as to why distance learning, which has been introduced in some parts of the world, has not reduced the psychological costs paid by children. The report makes it clear that distance learning supports some aspects of education but cannot replace them. Those that remain irreplaceable introduce the extremely high costs we have already discussed. Distance learning as well is, in the main, less effective. The report in question, describing the long-term effects, showed a decline in the quality of education by an average of 1.5 grades in a given subject (see also Andrabi et al., 2021; Marcotte & Hemelt, 2008) and a 0.19 standard deviation of math score (compared to the same exam administered during non-pandemic times, Maldonado & De Witte, 2021). Experiments in Brazil have shown outright that a group receiving online – as opposed to classroom – instruction covered as much as 75% less material (Lichand et al., 2021). Of particular importance, as a result of the pandemic, some children "dropped out" of the education system and never reentered school, which has long-term effects on their entire future lives (Bandiera et al., 2020). After all, the detrimental aspects of being undereducated need no explanation: among other things, reduced chances of high earnings, which, in turn, will be reflected in the quality of life of the next generation conceived by the COVID-19 pandemic generation.

The aforementioned report also revealed that school closures lead to an increase in educational inequalities, where higher-income families were less affected by the consequences of the pandemic for their children, as their resources allowed them to pay for other forms of education. A striking result from a study in the Netherlands showed that 55% of the effects/costs (losses) of school closures were concentrated around the 8% least educated families. Using a similar example, one can analyze the costs of school closures that lead to the inability to provide other education-related services. The report mentions that 388 million students benefit from school meals (which in many areas of the world is itself an incentive to send children to school). The pandemic triggered a decrease in the availability of meals for 370 million children, magnifying the poverty and food insecurity already affecting lower-income families at the outset. Against this backdrop, other long-term effects of the ongoing pandemic are clearly positioned. After all, what are the effects of child malnutrition? For example, the level of children's cognition and future school achievement drops (Fore et al., 2020). The COVID-19 pandemic particularly affects less privileged students who, in adulthood, will not be able to provide their children with the standard of living they would have achieved had there been no pandemic.

It has also been shown that 16% of girls and 8% of boys in Kenya did not return to school due to the COVID-19 lockdown (Presidential Policy and Strategic Unit and Population Council, 2021). Moreover, income projections show that schoolchildren affected by the COVID-19 pandemic will earn 17 trillion US dollars less over their lifetimes compared to what they would have earned had there been no pandemic (Abreh et al. 2021). Analogous losses are projected for preschool children at $308 billion (McCoy et al., 2021). This directly shows that the next generation – the children of today's children – will be affected by the lower parental incomes that were reduced by the COVID-19 pandemic! So the effects of the 2020–2022 pandemic (ending as we are concluding the writing of this book) will be permanently, tangibly, and materially felt for decades to come!

The report also indicates the long-term impact of this and future pandemics in that 96% of highly developed countries and only 16% of underdeveloped countries have implemented online learning. When we contrast this result with the continued problem of access to the Internet in underdeveloped countries (e.g., via cell phones, highly and moderately developed countries report that nearly 90% have cell phones in their homes, while underdeveloped countries report 17%), it is clear that the chasm between the situations of children from underdeveloped and highly developed countries will widen.

A similarly unfavorable contrast is revealed in the fact that 85% of highly developed and moderately developed countries provided support for teachers working online, while less than 30% of teachers received such assistance in underdeveloped ones. As a result, millions of teachers have incurred serious costs, not only professionally but also purely psychological in order to adjust to new working conditions. And teachers, after all, have their own families, themselves affected by the pandemic in this way as well.

In conclusion, the report under discussion above showed explicitly that closing (often first; before businesses) schools will exert a long-term effect on 1.6 billion children (UNESCO, 2021) and their capacity to develop through education while reducing their well-being and, finally, dramatically degrading their productivity. These losses are estimated to last for years, or even decades, while it is estimated that the broader business sector will recover its lost revenue much faster. The report's authors suggest methods to combat the psychological effects of future airborne pandemics: (1) prioritize the openness of schools (ahead of businesses; schools provide educational development but also, e.g., provide food); (2) focus on reducing infection in schools (e.g., by prioritizing vaccination of teachers); (3) support teachers in their ability and capacity to teach children. In short, the priority in pandemics should be to keep schools open at every stage of education for the reason that, in the long run, it is children who will be more affected by a pandemic than adults.

5.3 Neurological Impact = Years of Cognitive Dysfunctions

The last long-term change as an aftermath of COVID-19 is neurological changes leading to cognitive alterations. Let us note at the outset the multiplicity and breadth of brain areas that are affected by COVID-19 infection:

- Insula, cingulate cortex (Kandemirli et al., 2020)
- Olfactory nerve and gyrus rectus/straight gyrus (Petrescu et al., 2020)
- Gyrus rectus/straight gyrus and gyrus rectus/straight gyrus (Fischer et al., 2020)
- Thalamus (Fischer et al., 2020)
- Frontal, parietal, occipital lobe (Anzalone et al., 2020), bilateral medial temporal lobe, midbrain (Virhammar et al., 2020)

- Pons and corpus collosum (Zoghi et al., 2020)
- Left lateral orbitofrontal cortex, amygdala, hippocampus (Douaud et al., 2021)
- Cerebral peduncles and internal capsule (Zoghi et al., 2020)
- Internal capsule (Egbert et al., 2020)

The list above does not exhaust the range of neurological areas affected, as early data indicate that the COVID-19 virus affects the central nervous system (Yong, 2021), which may be associated with functional impairments (Cheng, Yang, Gao, 2020) and neurodegenerative conditions (Heneka et al., 2020). In young people who are not, after all, in the risk group for COVID-19 infection, deterioration of short-term and semantic memory, attention, and verbal learning difficulties have been observed even up to 3 months after infection (Woo et al., 2020). Other reported impairments include difficulty processing commands to perform simple motor activities (Helms et al., 2020), verbal memory impairment (Almeria et al., 2020) and working memory impairment (Hampshire et al., 2021), and cognitive slowing (Ferrucci et al., 2021) referred to as "post-COVID fog." Taken together, all of this means that the long-term neurological consequences will be very serious, permanently affecting the cognitive functioning of infected individuals.

In conclusion, it is clear that one of the few constant, unchanging features of the world around us is that in our perception it has threatened us, threatens us now, and will continue to threaten us. In addition to individual attacks from animals or other humans, we are menaced by weather disasters, volcanic eruptions, meteorite strikes, and, finally, disease. For centuries, these events have decimated not only *Homo sapiens* but all living creatures on earth. Therefore, it is safe to assume that in learning methods to avoid deadly threats, we have also evolved by developing the ability to cope with them. Unfortunately, the tools commonly applied in this struggle include the social cognition biases whose harmfulness we have written much about in this book. The following section is intended to illustrate the potential results of failing to respond to our deployment of these harmful mechanisms: the consequences of inaction will be felt for generations to come. And this, after all, is not the only threat facing us.

Final Remarks: It's Scary, but Manageable

We wrote this book at a time when optimists were proclaiming that the pandemic was dying out and pessimists were declaring that the mutated virus could still do mankind enormous harm. As psychologists, we will not pretend to know anything about virus mutations and epidemiology. Moreover, we don't know what the future holds with regard to the COVID-19 pandemic (however, by the time you hold this book in your hands, it may have become clear), although at the moment there seems to be little cause for optimism (sudden increase in cases in China, December 2022).

On the other hand, we can be certain that while our research program has identified several important regularities and opened up space for new questions and new research, we certainly wouldn't want another pandemic to serve as the springboard for investigating these issues. That said, we are aware that in this volume we have not exhausted all of the issues underlying the phenomenon of falsification of reality during the COVID-19 pandemic. You may feel a desire for more, which we fully understand. This is why, on multiple occasions in this book and for the last time here, we ask, encourage, and implore other researchers to take up the theme; it will perhaps allow us not only to successfully manage the current pandemic but also subsequent ones. And we must be prepared for the possibility that such an occasion will, unfortunately, arise again. Without waiting for this to happen, for the time being, we highlight what we have established:

1. Positive comparative illusions (in the form of better-than-average bias and unrealistic optimism) are common. They occur in various countries around the world, in diverse populations and during different pandemic periods.
2. The power of positive illusions is so great that they appear even in such populations where people should feel far more endangered than others.
3. Unrealistic optimism is a dangerous phenomenon, as it is associated with a lower (declared) propensity to follow health-promoting medical recommendations.
4. At the same time, unrealistic optimism turned out to be positively correlated with declared propensity to be vaccinated against COVID-19. Similarly, a positive relationship was noted for those declaring comparative pessimism, meaning

W. Kulesza, D. Doliński, *Social Biases During Covid 19*, SpringerBriefs in Psychology, https://doi.org/10.1007/978-3-031-34706-1

that people who are "unbiased," convinced that they are at the same at risk of contracting the disease as others, turned out to be the least likely to be vaccinated.

5. There are effective ways to reduce levels of unrealistic optimism both in the individual dimension (e.g., in doctor-patient contact) and at the collective level (e.g., through mass media).

However, we feel obliged to highlight here several limitations of the studies that we and other research teams have conducted during the pandemic. First of all, we note that the vast majority of such studies are based on verbal declarations by the participants. It is the respondents who tell us, the researchers, how often they wash their hands, how often they wear masks, or how much they avoid being in large groups of people (visiting movie theaters, attending concerts, etc.). This limitation is attributable to the period in which we had to conduct our research, forging a double-edged sword. On the one hand, we conducted research during a pandemic (the participants did not have to imagine "what would happen if they were in a pandemic"). On the other hand, we were conducting research in the middle of a pandemic, so the nature of the studies was such that we had no way of recording people's real-world behavior.

Therefore, we do not know whether the participants only seem to be prudent and disciplined or whether this is actually the case. It is also possible that they do not have such a good opinion of themselves and their behavior at all and are deliberately misleading us. They simply present themselves as decent and informed citizens because "it's the right thing to do." Wanting to make a good impression on the researchers, participants say what they think the researchers want to hear.

Occasionally, the situation becomes even more complicated. This is because sometimes we ask people not about their past or current behaviors but rather about their intentions for future – socially expected – behaviors. This was the case in numerous studies conducted when COVID-19 vaccines were not yet available, and the researchers asked people whether they would want to be vaccinated once it was possible. There are at least two methodological problems here. First, as before, we don't know whether the people declaring such a desire in our study actually have the intention to get vaccinated; and second, even if they do intend to do so at the time of the study, we don't know whether they will still have that intention once a vaccine is available. Maciuszek, Polak, and Stasiuk (2022) asked people about their intention to vaccinate against COVID-19 at the time when the vaccine was just being developed; next, after the vaccines had become available, they asked them whether they had vaccinated. It turned out that the relationship between the two phenomena was not very strong.

This is not to say that people's verbal declarations are not an important source of knowledge in scientific research. Of course they are! However, we must realize that they do not always necessarily coincide with real behavior. The caveats mentioned above, however, do not change the fact that the results of studies on comparative illusions accumulated by psychologists during the pandemic serve not only to expand psychological knowledge. We firmly believe that they can also be useful in designing interactions (e.g., global health policies) aimed at influencing other people to avoid unnecessary risks and manifest various health-promoting behaviors: getting screened, following a proper diet, or giving up smoking and reducing alcohol consumption. In turn, such interactions can take place both on a microscale (e.g., when one person persuades another to get vaccinated against the flu or do more physical exercise) and a macroscale (e.g., when an advertising agency works on a concept for a social campaign to persuade people to reduce their consumption of red meat or have screening tests done).

Looking at climate change, yielding adverse consequences in the form of sudden droughts (Somalia), floods (California), fires (Australia), as well as at geopolitical events (the invasion of Ukraine; North Korea's nuclear tests; unrest in Iran), and looking at changes in the growth of global health risks (not only the obvious increase in pandemic risks but, for example, the rise of antibiotic-resistant bacteria resulting from overuse of antibiotics), we can clearly see that research into how we cope psychologically with risks (sometimes severely and even fatally harming ourselves) is crucial. It is our hope that this small contribution to understanding emergencies and threatening mass events will also contribute to envisioning and designing a future in which we are not so much censors as we are scientists using knowledge for the common good.

Once, the Nobel Peace Prize laureate Lech Wałęsa, an electrician responsible for dismantling the Soviet Union and communist bloc in Europe, was asked in an interview about how to deal with some particular difficulties. Wałęsa, famously known for his quick and colorful wit, replied: "If you are afraid of a fever, just break the thermometer [in this case you won't have a temperature]."

And that is why we have written this book, so that you avoid breaking the thermometer, or at least not every time, and take a careful look at it. By doing so, you can avoid illness or other serious worries. Thank you, dear reader, for taking the time to read it.

References

Abreh, M. K., Agbevanu, W. K., Alhassan, A. J., Ansah, F., Bosu, R. S., Crawfurd, L., Milss, C.A., Minardi, A.L. & Nyame, G. (2021). *What happened to dropout rates after COVID-19 school closures in Ghana?* Center for Global Development. https://www.cgdev.org/blog/what-happened-dropout-rates-after-covid-19-school-closures-ghana

Alicke, M. D., Klotz, M. L., Breitenbecher, D. I., Yurak, T. J., & Vredenburg, D. S. (1995). Personal contact, individuation, and the better-than-average effect. *Journal of Personality and Social Psychology, 68*, 804–825.

Alloy, L. B., & Abramson, L. Y. (1979). The judgment of contigency in depressed and nondepressed students. Sadder but wiser? *Journal of Experimental Psychology: General, 108*, 441–485.

Almeria, M., Cejudo, J. C., Sotoca, J., Deus, J., & Krupinski, J. (2020). Cognitive profile following COVID-19 infection: Clinical predictors leading to neuropsychological impairment. *Brain, Behavior, and Immunity Health, 9*, 100163. https://doi.org/10.1016/j.bbih.2020.100163

Andrabi, T., Daniels, B., & Das, J. (2021). Human capital accumulation and disasters: Evidence from the Pakistan earthquake of 2005. *RISE Working Paper Series. 20/039*. https://doi.org/10.35489/BSG-RISE-WP_2020/039. https://riseprogramme.org/publications/human-capital-accumulation-and-disasters-evidence-pakistanearthquake-2005.

Anzalone, N., Castellano, A., Scotti, R., Scandroglio, A. M., Filippi, M., Ciceri, F., et al. (2020). Multifocal laminar cortical brain lesions: A consistent MRI finding in neuro-COVID-19 patients. *Journal of Neurology, 267*(10), 2806–2809. https://doi.org/10.1007/s00415-020-09966-2

Aranguren, M. (2022). Face mask use conditionally decreases compliance with physical distancing rules against COVID-19: Gender differences in risk compensation pattern. *Annals of Behavioral Medicine, 56*(4), 332–346.

Armor, D. A., & Taylor, S. E. (2003). The effects of mindset on behavior: Self-regulation in deliberative and implemental frames of mind. *Personality and Social Psychology Bulletin, 29*, 86–95.

Asendorpf, J. B., & Ostendoerf, F. (1998). Is self-enhancement healthy? Conceptual, psychometric, and empirical analysis. *Journal of Personality and Social Psychology, 74*, 955–966.

Asimakopoulou, K., Hoorens, V., Speed, E., Coulson, N. S., Antoniszczak, D., Collyer, F., Deschrijver, E., Dubbin, L., Faulks, D., Foryth, R., Harslof, I., Larsen, K., Manaras, I., Olczak-Kowalczyk, D., Willis, K., Xenou, T., & Scambler, S. (2020). Comparative optimism about infection and recovery from COVID-19; implications for adherence with lockdown advice. *Health Expectations, 23*, 1502–1511.

Bandiera, O., Buehren, N., Goldstein, M., Rasul, I., & Smurra, A. (2020). Do school closures during an epidemic have persistent effects? Evidence from Sierra Leone in the time of Ebola: Working Paper UCL.https://www.povertyactionlab.org/sites/default/files/research-paper/workingpaper_720_School-Closures-During-Epidemic_Sierra-Leone_July2020.pdf..

W. Kulesza, D. Doliński, *Social Biases During Covid 19*, SpringerBriefs in Psychology, https://doi.org/10.1007/978-3-031-34706-1

Baumeister, R. F. (1989). The optimal margin of illusion. *Journal of Social and Clinical Psychology, 8*, 176–189.

Bonanno, G. A., Rennicke, C., & Dekel, S. (2005). Self-enhancement among high-exposure survivors of the September 11th terrorist attack: Resilience or social maladjustment? *Journal of Personality and Social Psychology, 88*, 984–998.

Boyd-Wilson, B. M., McClure, J., & Walkey, F. M. (2004). Are wellbeing and illusory perceptions linked? The answer may be yes, but.... *Australian Journal of Psychology, 56*, 1–9.

Brooking, J. B., & Serratelli, A. J. (2006). Positive illusions: Positive correlated with subjective well-being, negatively correlated with a measure of personal growth. *Psychological Reports, 98*, 407–413.

Brown, J. D. (1986). Evaluations of self and others: Self-enhancement biases in social judgments. *Social Cognition, 4*, 353–376.

Brown, J. D. (2012). Understanding the better than average effect: Motives (still) matter. *Personality and Social Psychology Bulletin, 38*(2), 209–219.

Browning, M. H. E. M., Larson, L. R., Sharaievska, I., Rigolon, A., McAnirlin, O., Mullenbach, L., et al. (2021). Psychological impacts from COVID-19 among university students: Risk factors across seven states in the United States. *PLoS One, 16*(1), e0245327.

Burger, J. M., & Burns, L. (1988). The illusion of unique invulnerability and the use of effective contraception. *Personality and Social Psychology Bulletin, 14*, 264–270.

Burger, J. M., & Palmer, M. L. (1992). Changes in and generalization of unrealistic optimism following experiences with stressful events: Reactions to the 1989 California earthquake. *Personality and Social Psychology Bulletin, 18*(1), 39–43.

Byram, S. J. (1997). Cognitive and motivational factors influencing time prediction. *Journal of Experimental Psychology: Applied, 3*, 216–239.

Byrnes, J. P., Miller, D. C., & Schafer, W. D. (1999). Gender differences in risk taking: A meta-analysis. *Psychological Bulletin, 125*(3), 367–383.

Cai, X., Hu, X., Ekumi, I. O., Wang, J., An, Y., Li, Z., & Yuan, B. (2020). Psychological distress and its correlates among COVID-19 survivors during early convalescence across age groups. *The American Journal of Geriatric Psychiatry, 28*(10), 1030–1039. https://doi.org/10.1016/j.jagp.2020.07.003

Calderon, T. G. (1993). Predictive properties of analysts' forecasts of corporate earnings. *The Mid-Atlantic Journal of Business, 29*, 41–58.

Castelli, L., Pavan, G., Ferrari, E., & Kashima, Y. (2009). The stereotyper and the chameleon: The effects of stereotype use on perceivers' mimicry. *Journal of Experimental Social Psychology, 45*(4), 835–839. https://doi.org/10.1016/j.jesp.2009.02.012

Chambers, J. R., & Windschitl, P. D. (2004). Biases in social comparative judgments: The role of nonmotivated factors in above-average and comparative-optimism effects. *Psychological Bulletin, 130*(5), 813–838.

Chambers, J. R., Windschitl, P. D., & Suls, J. (2003). Egocentrism, event frequency, and comparative optimism: When what happens frequently is "more likely to happen to me". *Personality and Social Psychology Bulletin, 29*, 1343–1356.

Cheng, Q., Yang, Y., & Gao, J. (2020). Infectivity of human coronavirus in the brain. *eBioMedicine, 56*, 102799. https://doi.org/10.1016/j.ebiom.2020.102799

Chrystal, P. (2021). *The history of the world in 100 pandemics, plagues and epidemics*. Pen and Sword History.

Clair, R., Gordon, M., Kroon, M., & Reilly, C. (2021). The effects of social isolation on well-being and life satisfaction during pandemic. *Humanities and Social Sciences Communications, 8*(1), 1–6.

Clarke, V. A., Lovegrove, H., Williams, A., & Machperson, M. (2000). Unrealistic optimism and the Health Belief Model. *Journal of Behavioral Medicine, 23*(4), 367–376. https://doi.org/10.1023/A:1005500917875

Collard, J. J., Cummins, R. A., & Fuller-Tyskiewicz, M. (2016). Measurement of positive irrational beliefs (positive cognitive illusions). *Journal of Happiness Studies: An Interdisciplinary Forum on Subjective Well-Being, 17*, 1069–1088.

Courtenay, W. H. (2000). Behavioral factors associated with disease, injury, and death among men: Evidence and implications for prevention. *The Journal of Men's Studies, 9*(1), 81–142.

Crocker, J., & Gallo, L. (1985). *The self-enhancing effect of downward comparison*. Paper presented at the annual meeting of American Psychological Association, Los Angeles.

Cross, K. P. (1977). Not can, but will college teaching be improved? *New Directions for Higher Education, 17*, 1–15.

Dalrymple, K. E., & Scheufele, D. A. (2007). Finally informing the electorate? How the internet got people thinking about presidential politics in 2004. *Harvard International Journal of Press/Politics, 12*(3), 96–111.

Davide, P., Andrea, P., Martina, O., Andrea, E., Davide, D., & Mario, A. (2020). The impact of the COVID-19 pandemic on patients with OCD: Effects of contamination symptoms and remission state before the quarantine in a preliminary naturalistic study. *Psychiatry Research, 291*, 113213. https://doi.org/10.1016/j.psychres.2020.113213

Davidson, K., & Prkachin, K. (1997). Optimism and unrealistic optimism have an interacting impact on health-promoting behavior and knowledge changes. *Personality and Social Psychology Bulletin, 23*(6), 617–625.

Debowska, A., Horeczy, B., Boduszek, D., & Dolinski, D. (2022). A repeated cross-sectional survey assessing university students' stress, depression, anxiety, and suicidality in the early stages of the COVID-19 pandemic in Poland. *Psychological Medicine, 52*, 3744–3747. https://doi.org/10.1017/S003329172000392X

Dewberry, C & Richardson, S. (1990). Effect of Anxiety on Optimism. *The Journal of Social Psychology, 130*(6,) 731–738. https://doi.org/10.1080/00224545.1990.9924625 https://www.tandfonline.com/doi/abs/10.1080/00224545.1990.99246

Dillard, A. J., McCaul, K. D., & Klein, W. M. (2006). Unrealistic optimism in smokers: Implications for smoking myth endorsement and self-protective motivation. *Journal of Health Community, 11*, 93–102.

Dillard, A. J., Midboe, A. M., & Klein, W. M. (2009). The dark side of optimism: Unrealistic optimism about problems with alcohol predicts subsequent negative event experiences. *Personality and Social Psychology Bulletin, 35*, 1540–1550.

Dolinski, D. (2018). Is psychology still a science of behaviour? *Social Psychological Bulletin, 13*(2), 1–14. https://doi.org/10.5964/spb.v13i2.25025

Dolinski, D., & Gromski, W. (1987). *(Unrealistic) optimism is back* (Working paper). Opole, Poland.

Dolinski, D., & Grzyb, T. (2020). *The social psychology of obedience towards authority: An empirical tribute to Stanley Milgram*. Routledge.

Dolinski, D., Gromski, W., & Zawisza, E. (1987). Unrealistic pessimism. *Journal of Social Psychology, 127*, 511–516.

Dolinski, D., Dolinska, B., Zmaczynska-Witek, B., Banach, M., & Kulesza, W. (2020). Unrealistic optimism in the time of coronavirus pandemic: May it help to kill, if so – Whom: Disease or the person? *Journal of Clinical Medicine, 9*, 1464.

Dolinski, D., Kulesza, W., Muniak, P., Dolinska, B., Derakshan, A., & Grzyb, T. (2021). Research on unrealistic optimism among HoReCa workers as a possible future hotspot of infections. *Sustainability, 13*, 12562.

Dolinski, D., Kulesza, W., Muniak, P., Dolinska, D., Węgrzyn, R., & Izydorczak, K. (2022). Media intervention program for reducing unrealistic optimism bias: The link between unrealistic optimism, well-being, and health. *Applied Psychology: Health and Well Being, 14*(2), 499–518.

Douaud, G., Lee, S., Alfaro-Almagro, F., Arthofer, C., Wang, C., Lange, F., et al. (2021). Brain imaging before and after COVID-19 in UK biobank. *MedRxiv: The Preprint Server for Health Sciences, 2021*(06), 11.21258690. https://doi.org/10.1101/2021.06.11.21258690

Druică, E., Musso, F., & Ianole-Călin, R. (2020). Optimism bias during the Covid-19 pandemic: Empirical evidence from Romania and Italy. *Games, 11*(3), 39.

Dufner, M., Gevbauer, J. E., Sedikides, C., & Denissen, J. J. A. (2019). Self-enhancement and psychological adjustment: A meta-analytic review. *Personality and Social Psychology Review, 23*, 48–72.

Dunning, D., Meyerowitz, J. A., & Holzberg, A. D. (1989). Ambiguity and self-evaluation: The role of idiosyncratic trait definitions in self-serving assessments of ability. *Journal of Personality and Social Psychology, 57*, 1082–1090.

Egbert, A. R., Cankurtaran, S., & Karpiak, S. (2020). Brain abnormalities in COVID-19 acute/subacute phase: A rapid systematic review. *Brain, Behavior, and Immunity, 89*, 543–554. https://doi.org/10.1016/j.bbi.2020.07.014

Epley, N., & Dunning, D. (2000). Feeling "holier than thou": Are self-serving assessments produced by errors in self-or social prediction? *Journal of Personality and Social Psychology, 79*(6), 861–875.

Eveland, W. P., Seo, M., & Marton, K. (2002). Learning from the news in campaign 2000: An experimental comparison of TV news, newspapers, and online news. *Media Psychology, 4*(4), 353–378.

Ferrucci, R., Dini, M., Groppo, E., Rosci, C., Reitano, M. R., Bai, F., et al. (2021). Long-lasting cognitive abnormalities after COVID-19. *Brain Sciences, 11*(2), 235. https://doi.org/10.3390/brainsci11020235

Festinger, L. (1954). A theory of social comparison processes. *Human Relations, 7*, 117–140.

Figueiras, M. J., Neto, D. D., Maroco, J., & Kern de Castro, E. (2022). *Is my risk lower than yours? The role of compared risk, illness perceptions, and self-efficacy as determinants of perceived risk for COVID-19* (Vol. 24, pp. 1–13). Health Risk and Society.

Fischer, D., Threlkeld, Z. D., Bodien, Y. G., Kirsch, J. E., Huang, S. Y., Schaefer, P. W., et al. (2020). Intact brain network function in an unresponsive patient with COVID-19. *Annals of Neurology, 88*(4), 851–854. https://doi.org/10.1002/ana.25838

Fore, H. H., Dongyu, Q., Beasley, D. M., & Ghebreyesus, T. A. (2020). Child malnutrition and COVID-19: The time to act is now. *The Lancet (British Edition), 396*(10250), 517–518.

Global Education Evidence Advisory Panel. (2022). *Prioritizing learning during COVID-19: The most effective ways to keep children learning during and post- pandemic* [K. Akyeampong, T. Andrabi, A. Banerjee, R. Banerji, S. Dynarski, R. Glennerster, S. Grantham-McGregor, K. Muralidharan, B. Piper, S. Ruto, J. Saavedra, S. Schmelkes, & H. Yoshikawa]. The World Bank, FCDO, and UNICEF Office of Research – Innocenti.

Goethals, G. R. (1986). Fabricating and ignoring social reality: Self-serving estimates of consensus. In J. M. Olson, C. P. Herman, & M. P. Zanna (Eds.), *Relative deprivation and social comparison: The Ontario symposium* (Vol. 4, pp. 137–157). Erlbaum.

Gollwitzer, P. M. (1996). The volitional benefits of planning. In P. M. Gollwitzer & J. A. Bargh (Eds.), *The psychology of action. Linking cognition and motivation to behavior* (pp. 287–312). Guilford Press.

Gollwitzer, P. M. (2003). Why we thought that action mind-set affect illusions of control. *Psychological Inquiry, 14*, 261–269.

Gollwitzer, P. M., & Kinney, R. F. (1989). Effect of deliberative and implemental mind-sets on illusion of control. *Journal of Personality and Social Psychology, 56*, 531–542.

Greenwald, A. G. (1980). The totalitarian ego. Fabrication and revision of personal history. *American Psychologist, 35*, 603–618.

Gregg, A. P., Mahaderan, N., & Sedikides, C. (2017). The SPOT effect: People spontaneously prefer their own theories. *Quarterly Journal of Experimental Psychology, 70*(6), 996–1010.

Griffin, D., & Buehler, R. (1999). Frequency, probability, and prediction: Easy solutions to cognitive illusions? *Cognitive Psychology, 38*, 48–78.

Gros, D. F., Flanagan, J. C., Korte, K. J., Mills, A. C., Brady, K. T., & Back, S. E. (2016). Relations between social support, PTSD symptoms, and substance use in veterans. *Psychology of Addictive Behaviors, 30*(7), 764–770.

Grosser, T. J., Gilson, L. L., Dong, Y., & Madjar, N. (2021). Creative self-enhancement in a team context: The role of gender, creative self-concept, and trait hypercompetitiveness. *Psychology of Aesthetic, Creativity, and the Arts*. https://doi.org/10.1037/aca0000430

Gruder, C. L. (1971). Determinants of social comparison choices. *Journal of Experimental Social Psychology, 7*, 473–489.

Grzyb, T., & Dolinski, D. (2017). Beliefs about obedience levels in studies conducted within the Milgram paradigm. Better than average effect and comparisons of typical behaviors by representatives of various nations. *Frontiers in Psychology, 8*, 1632.

Hahmiller, K. L. (1966). Threat as a determinant of downward comparison. *Journal of Experimental Social Psychology, 2*(Suppl 1), 32–39.

Hampshire, A., Trender, W., Chamberlain, S. R., Jolly, A. E., Grant, J. E., Patrick, F., et al. (2021). Cognitive deficits in people who have recovered from COVID-19. *EClinicalMedicine, 39*, 101044. https://doi.org/10.1016/j.eclinm.2021.101044

Hanoch, Y., Rolinson, J., & Freund, A. M. (2019). Reaping the benefits and avoiding the risk: Unrealistic optimism in the health domain. *Risk Analysis, 39*(4), 792–804.

Hanoch, Y., Simuzingili, M., & Barnes, A. (2022). The role of unrealistic absolute optimism in willingness to be treated and pay for medical services. *Decision*. https://doi.org/10.1037/dec0000184

Hart, W., Albarracin, D., Eagly, A. H., Brehan, J., Lindberg, M. J., & Merill, L. (2009). Feeling validated versus being correct: A meta-analysis of selective exposure to information. *Psychological Bulletin, 135*(4), 558–588.

Harris, P., Griffin, D., & Murray, S. (2008). Testing the limits of optimistic bias: Event and person moderators in a multilevel framework. *Journal of Personality and Social Psychology, 95*(5), 1225–1237. doi: 10.1037/a0013315

Helms, J., Kremer, S., Merdji, H., Clere-Jehl, R., Schenck, M., Kummerlen, C., et al. (2020). Neurologic features in severe SARS-CoV-2 infection. *The New England Journal of Medicine, 382*(23), 2268–2270. https://doi.org/10.1056/NEJMc2008597

Helweg-Larsen, M. (1999). (The lack of) optimistic biases in response to the 1994 Northridge Earthquake: The role of personal experience. *Basic and Applied Social Psychology, 21*, 119–129.

Helweg-Larsen, M., & Shepperd, J. A. (2001). Do moderators of the optimistic bias affect personal or target risk estimates? A review of the literature. *Personality and Social Psychology Review, 5*, 74–95.

Heneka, M. T., Golenbock, D., Latz, E., Morgan, D., & Brown, R. (2020). Immediate and long-term consequences of COVID-19 infections for the development of neurological disease. *Alzheimer's Research and Therapy, 12*(1), 69. https://doi.org/10.1186/s13195-020-00640-3

Hoorens, V. (1995). Self-favoring biases, self-presentation, and the self-other asymmetry in social comparison. *Journal of Personality, 63*(4), 793–817.

Hoorens, V., & Buunk, B. P. (1993). Social comparison of health risks: Locus of control, the person-positivity bias, and unrealistic optimism. *Journal of Applied Social Psychology, 23*, 291–302.

Hoorens, V., & Smits, T. (2001). Why do controllabe events elicit stronger comparative optimism than uncontrollable events? *Revue Internationale de Psychologie Sociale, 14*, 11–43.

Hoorens, V., Scambler, S., Deschrijver, E., Coulson, N. S., Speed, E., & Asimakopoulou, K. (2022). Comparative optimism, self superiority, egocentric impact perception and health information seeking: A COVID-19 study. *Psychologica Belgica, 62*(1), 152–167.

Horney, K. (1937). *The neurotic personality of our time*. Norton.

Huang, Y., & Zhao, N. (2020). Generalized anxiety disorder, depressive symptoms and sleep quality during COVID-19 outbreak in China: A web-based cross-sectional survey. *Psychiatry Research, 288*, 112954. https://doi.org/10.1016/j.psychres.2020.112954

Idoiaga, N., Berasategi, N., Eiguren, A., & Picaza, M. (2020). Exploring children's social and emotional representations of the Covid-19 pandemic. *Frontiers in Psychology, 11*, 1952.

Irwin, F. W. (1953). Stated expectations as functions of probability and desirability of outcomes. *Journal of Personality, 21*, 329–335.

Izydorczak, K., Antoniuk, K., Kulesza, W., Muniak, P., & Dolinski, D. (2022). Temporal aspects of unrealistic optimism and robustness of this bias: A longitudinal study in the context of the COVID-19 pandemic. *PLoS One, 17*(12), e0278045. https://doi.org/10.1371/journal.pone.0278045

Izydorczak, K., Dolinski, D., Genschow, O., Kulesza, W., Muniak, P., Casara, B., & Suitner, C. (2023). *Do unbiased people act more rationally? The case of comparative realism and vaccine intention*. Royal Society Open Science. (in press).

Jelic, M. (2022). How do we process feedback? The role of self-esteem in processing self-related and other-related information. *Acta Psychologica, 227*, 103592.

Jellison, J., & Davis, D. (1973). Relationship between perceived ability and attitude extremity. *Journal of Personality and Social Psychology, 27*, 430–436.

Kahneman, D., & Tversky, A. (1979). Prospect theory: An empirical analysis of decision under risk. *Econometrica, 47*(2), 263–292.

Kandemirli, S. G., Dogan, L., Sarikaya, Z. T., Kara, S., Akinci, C., Kaya, D., et al. (2020). Brain MRI findings in patients in the intensive care unit with COVID-19 infection. *Radiology, 297*(1), E232–E235. https://doi.org/10.1148/radiol.2020201697

Kim, M. Y., & Han, K. (2022). For me or for others? The better-than-average effect and negative feelings toward average others during the COVID-19 pandemic. *Current Psychology*. https://doi.org/10.1007/s12144-021-02548-z

Kim, H. K., & Niederdeppe, J. (2013). Exploring optimistic bias and the integrative model of behavioral prediction in the context of a campus influenza outbreak. *Journal of Health Communication, 18*(2), 206–222.

Kim, H. K., & Niederdeppe, J. (2016). Effects of self-affirmation, narratives, and informational messages in reducing unrealistic optimism about alcohol-related problems among college students. *Human Communication Research, 42*(2), 246–268.

Kinney, A. (2000). Positive illusions of well-being and irrational implications for rational-emotive behavior therapy. *Journal of Contemporary Psychotherapy: On the Cutting Edge of Modern Developments in Psychotherapy, 30*(4), 401–415.

Klein, C., & Helweg-Larsen, M. (2002). Perceived control and the optimistic bias: A meta-analytic review. *Psychology and Health, 17*(4), 437–446.

Klein, W. M., & Weinstein, N. D. (1997). Social comparison and unrealistic optimism about personal risk. In B. P. Buunk & F. X. Gibbons (Eds.), *Health, coping, and well-being: Perspectives from social comparison theory* (pp. 25–61). Lawrence Erlbaum Associates Publishers.

Koole, S., & Spijker, M. (2000). Overcoming the planning fallacy through willpower: Effects of implementation intentions on actual and predicted task-completion times. *European Journal of Social Psychology, 30*, 873–888.

Korman, A. L. (1976). Hypothesis of work behavior revisited and an extension. *Academy of Management Review, 1*, 50–63.

Kruger, J. (1999). Lake Wobegon be gone! The "below average effect" and the egocentric nature of comparative ability judgments. *Journal of Personality and Social Psychology, 77*, 221–232.

Kulesza, W., Dolinski, D., Huisman, A., & Majewski, R. (2014). The echo effect: The power of verbal mimicry to influence prosocial behavior. *Journal of Language and Social Psychology, 33*(2), 183–201. https://doi.org/10.1177/0261927x13506906

Kulesza, W., Dolinski, D., Muniak, P., Derakhshan, A., Rizulla, A., & Banach, M. (2020). We are infected with the new, mutated virus UO-COVID-19. *Archives of Medical Science, 17*, 1706–1715.

Kulesza, W., Dolinski, D., Muniak, P., Grzyb, T., & Rizulla, A. (2022a). COVID-19 and a biased public mentality toward infection and vaccination: A case of unrealistic optimism and social comparisons between the vaccinated and unvaccinated. *Journal of Pacific Rim Psychology, 16*, 1–7.

Kulesza, W., Dolinski, D., Muniak, P., Winner, D., Izydorczak, K., Derakhshan, A., & Rizulla, A. (2022b). Biased social comparison in the moment of crisis: The better-than-average effect and COVID-19. *Social Psychology*. https://doi.org/10.1027/1864-9335/a000495

Kulesza, W., Dolinski, D., Muniak, P., & Rizulla, A. (2023a). Mimicry boosts social bias: Unrealistic optimism in a health prevention case. *Social Influence*. (in press).

Kulesza, W., Dolinski, D., Suitner, C., Genschow, O., Muniak, P., Izydorczak, K., & Salvador, C. B. G. (2023b). It matters to whom you compare yourself: The case of unrealistic optimism and gender-specific comparisons. *American Journal of Men's Health*. (in press).

Kulesza, W., Dolinski, D., Muniak, P, Izydorczak, K., Kozłowska, P., Mazurkiewicz, W., & Rizulla, A. (2023c). 3-6-9 "Threatened-me" rule: Testing a new method to reduce unrealistic optimism. Manuscript under review.

Kumar, A., & Somani, A. (2020). Dealing with Corona virus anxiety and OCD. *Asian Journal of Psychiatry, 51*, 102053. https://doi.org/10.1016/j.ajp.2020.102053

Kupier-Smith, B. J., Doppelhofer, L., Oganian, Y., Rosenblau, G., & Korn, C. (2021). Optimistic beliefs about the personal impact of COVID-19 pandemic. *Royal Society Open Science, 8*, 210904210904. https://doi.org/10.1098/rsos.210904

Lakin, J. L., Chartrand, T. L., & Arkin, R. M. (2008). I am too just like you: Nonconscious mimicry as an automatic behavioral response to social exclusion. *Psychological Science, 19*(8), 816–822. https://doi.org/10.1111/j.1467-9280.2008.02162.x

Langer, E. J. (1975). The illusion of control. *Journal of Personality and Social Psychology, 32*, 311–328.

Latané, B. (1966). Studies in social comparison – Introduction and overview. *Journal of Experimental Social Psychology, 2*(Suppl 1), 1–5.

Leary, M. (2007). Motivational and emotional aspects of the self. *Annual Review of Psychology, 58*, 317–344.

Lee, J. (2012). Trait desirability and cultural difference in the better-than-average effect. *Asian Journal of Social Psychology, 15*(4), 261–272.

Leighton, J., Bird, G., Orsini, C., & Heyes, C. (2010). Social attitudes modulate automatic imitation. *Journal of Experimental Social Psychology, 46*(6), 905–910. https://doi.org/10.1016/j.jesp.2010.07.001

Lemyre, L., & Smith, P. L. (1985). Intergroup discrimination and self-esteem in the minimal intergroup paradigm. *Journal of Personality and Social Psychology, 49*, 660–670.

Leviston, Z., & Uren, H. V. (2020). Overestimating one's "green" behavior: Better-than-average bias may function to reduce perceived personal threat from climate change. *The Journal of Social Issues, 76*(1), 70–85.

Lichand, G., Dória, C. A., Neto, O. L., & Cossi, J. (2021). The impacts of remote learning in secondary education: Evidence from Brazil during the pandemic. Inter-American Development Bank: São Paulo, Brazil. https://doi.org/10.21203/rs.3.rs-568605/v1

Lin, T., Harris, E. A., Heemskerk, A., Van Bavel, J. J., & Ebner, N. C. (2021). A multi-national test on self-reported compliance with COVID-19 public health measures: The role of individual age and gender demographics and countries' developmental status. *Social Science and Medicine, 286*, 114335.

Linkenbach, J., & Perkins, H. W. (2005). *Montana's MOST of us don't drink & drive campaign: A social norms strategy to reduce impaired driving among 21 to 34 year olds: (624262011–001)* [data set]. American Psychological Association.

Maciuszek, J., Polak, M., & Stasiuk, K. (2022). Declared intention (not) to be vaccinated against COVID-19, and actual behavior – The longitudinal study in the polish sample. *Vaccine, 10*(2), 147.

Maftei, A., & Petroi, C. E. (2022). "I'm luckier than everybody else": Optimistic bias, COVID-19 conspiracy beliefs, vaccination status, and the link with the time spent online, anticipated regret, and the perceived threat. *Frontiers in Public Health, 10*, 1019298.

Mahalik, J. R., Lagan, H. D., & Morrison, J. A. (2006). Health behaviors and masculinity in Kenyan and U.S. male college students. *Psychology of Men and Masculinity, 7*(4), 191–202.

Mak, I. W. C., Chu, C. M., Pan, P. C., Yiu, M. G. C., & Chan, V. L. (2009). Long-term psychiatric morbidities among SARS survivors. *General Hospital Psychiatry, 31*(4), 318–326. https://doi.org/10.1016/j.genhosppsych.2009.03.001

Maksim, A., Spiewak, S., Lipp, N., Duzmanska-Misiarczyk, N., Gustaw, G., Rebilas, K., & Strojny, P. (2022). *Unrealistic optimism in the eye of the storm: Positive bias towards the consequences of COVID-19 during the second and third waves of the pandemic*. medRxiv preprint. https://doi.org/10.1101/2022.05.10.22274918

Maldonado, J. E., & De Witte, K. (2021). The effect of school closures on standardised student test outcomes. *British Educational Research Journal*. https://doi.org/10.1002/berj.3754

Marcotte, D. E., & Hemelt, S. W. (2008). Unscheduled school closings and student performance. *Education Finance and Policy, 3*(3), 316–338.

Marks, R. W. (1951). The effect of probability, desirability and "privilege" on the stated expectation of children. *Journal of Personality, 19*, 332–351. https://doi.org/10.1111/j.1467-6494.1951.tb01107.x

Maslow, A. H. (1954). *Motivation and personality*. Harper.

Matlin, M. W., & Stang, D. J. (1978). *The Pollyanna principle. Selectivity in language, memory, and thought*. Schenkman Publishing Company.

Mazza, M. G., De Lorenzo, R., Conte, C., Poletti, S., Vai, B., Bollettini, I., et al. (2020). Anxiety and depression in COVID-19 survivors: Role of inflammatory and clinical predictors. *Brain, Behavior, and Immunity, 89*, 594–600. https://doi.org/10.1016/j.bbi.2020.07.037

McCaul, K. D., Branstetter, A. D., Schroeder, D. M., & Glasgow, R. E. (1996). What is the relationship between breast cancer risk and mammography screening? A meta-analytic review. *Health Psychology, 15*, 423–492.

McColl, K., Debin, M., Souty, C., Guerrisi, C., Turbelin, C., Falchi, A., Bonmarin, I., Paolotti, D., Obi, C., Duggan, J., Moreno, Y., Wisniak, A., Flahault, A., Blanchon, T., Colizza, V., & Raude, J. (2022). Are people optimistically biased about the risk of COVID-19 infection? Lessons from the first wave of the pandemic in Europe. *International Journal of Environmental Research and Public Health, 19*, 436.

McCoy, D. C., Cuartas, J., Behrman, J., Cappa, C., Heymann, J., López Bóo, F., et al. (2021). Global estimates of the implications of COVID-19-related preprimary school closures for children's instructional access, development, learning, and economic wellbeing. *Child Development, 92*(5), e883–e899.

McKenna, F. P. (1993). It won't happen to me: Unrealistic optimism or illusion of control? *British Journal of Psychology, 84*, 39–50.

McKenna, F. P., & Albery, I. P. (2001). Does unrealistic optimism change following a negative experience? *Journal of Applied Social Psychology, 31*(6), 1146–1157.

McMillen, C. (2016). *Pandemic: A very short introduction*. Oxford University Press.

Meisner, M. W., Lenzenweger, M. F., Bach, B., Vestergaard, M., Petersen, L. S., Haahr, U. H., Kongerslev, M., & Simonsen, E. (2021). Exploring identity disturbance and psychotic spectrum symptoms as predictors of borderline and schizotypal personality disorders. *Psychopathology, 54*, 193–202.

Menon, G., Kyung, E. J., & Agrawal, N. (2009). Biases in social comparisons: Optimism or pessimism? *Organizational Behavior and Human Decision Process, 108*, 39–52.

Meyer, W. G. (2014). The effect of optimism bias on the decision to terminate failing projects. *Project Management Journal, 45*(4), 7–20.

Milgram, S. (1963). Behavioral study of obedience. *Journal of Abnormal Psychology, 67*, 371–378.

Milgram, S. (1965). Some conditions of obedience and disobedience to authority. *Human Relations, 18*, 57–76.

Milgram, S. (1974). *Obedience to authority. An experimental view*. Harper & Row.

Moore, D. A., & Healy, P. J. (2008). The trouble with overconfidence. *Psychological Review, 115*, 502–517.

O'Creery, M. F., Nicholson, N., Soane, M., & Willman, P. (2010). Tranding on illusions: Unrealistic perceptions of control and tranding performance. *Journal of Occupational and Organizational Psychology, 76*, 53–68.

O'Hare, D. (1990). Pilots' perception of risks and hazards in general aviation. *Aviation, Space, and Environmental Medicine, 61*, 599–603.

Ochse, C. (2012). The optimism bias: Is it adaptive in academic settings? *Journal of Psychology in Africa, 22*(3), 415–417.

Oljača, M., Sadiković, S., Branovački, B., Pajić, D., Smederevac, S., & Mitrović, D. (2020). Unrealistic optimism and XECAXO traits as predictors of risk perception and compliance with COVID-19 preventive measures during the first wave of pandemic. *Primenjena Psychologija, 13*(4), 405–425.

Orwell, G. (1949/2021). *1984*. Intra.

Pahl, S., & Eiser, J. R. (2007). How malleable is comparative self-positivity? The effects of manipulating judgmental focus and accessibility. *European Journal of Social Psychology, 37*, 617–627.

Park, T., Ju, I., Ohs, J. E., & Hinsley, A. (2021). Optimistic bias and preventive behavioral engagement in the context of COVID-19. *Research in Social and Administrative Pharmacy, 17*(1), 1859–1866.

Parker, A. M., Sricharoenchai, T., Raparla, S., Schneck, K. W., Bienvenu, O. J., & Needham, D. M. (2015). Posttraumatic stress disorder in critical illness survivors: A metaanalysis. *Critical Care Medicine, 43*(5), 1121–1129. https://doi.org/10.1097/CCM.0000000000000882

Perloff, L. S. (1983). Perceptions of vulnerability to victimization. *Journal of Social Issues, 39*, 41–61.

Perloff, L. S., & Fetzer, B. K. (1986). Self–other judgments and perceived vulnerability to victimization. *Journal of Personality and Social Psychology, 50*(3), 502–510.

Petrescu, A. M., Taussig, D., & Bouilleret, V. (2020). Electroencephalogram (EEG) in COVID-19: A systematic retrospective study. *Neurophysiologie Clinique/Clinical Neurophysiology, 50*(3), 155–165. https://doi.org/10.1016/j.neucli.2020.06.001

Pieri, E. (2021). *Pandemics. The basics*. Routledge.

Prati, G. (2021). Mental health and its psychosocial predictors during national quarantine in Italy against the coronavirus disease 2019 (COVID-19). *Anxiety, Stress, and Coping, 34*(2), 145–156. https://doi.org/10.1080/10615806.2020.1861253

Prati, G., & Mancini, A. (2021). The psychological impact of COVID-19 pandemic lockdowns: A review and meta-analysis of longitudinal studies and natural experiments. *Psychological Medicine, 51*(2), 201–211. https://doi.org/10.1017/S0033291721000015

Presidential Policy and Strategic Unit & Population Council. (2021). *Promises to keep: The impact of COVID-19 on adolescents in Kenya*. https://knowledgecommons.popcouncil.org/departments_sbsr-pgy/1334/

Puca, R. M. (2001). Preferred difficulty and subjective probability in different action phases. *Motivation and Emotion, 25*, 307–326.

Rothman, A. J., Klein, W. M., & Weinstein, N. D. (1996). Absolute and relative biases in estimations of personal risk. *Journal of Applied Social Psychology, 26*(14), 1213–1236.

Ruthig, J. C., Gamblin, B. W., Jones, K., Vanderzanden, K., & Kehn, A. (2017). Concurrently examining unrealistic absolute and comparative optimism: Temporal shifts, individual difference and event-specific correlates, and behavioural outcome. *British Journal of Psychology, 108*, 107–126.

Salgado, S., & Berntsen, D. (2021). "It won't happen to us": Unrealistic optimism affects COVID-19 risk assessments and attitudes regarding protective behaviour. *Journal of Applied Research in Memory and Cognition, 10*, 368–380.

Savage M. J., James R., Magistro D., Donaldson J., Healy L. C., Nevill M., Hennis P. J. (2020). Mental health and movement behaviour during the COVID-19 pandemic in UK university students: Prospective cohort study. *Mental Health and Physical Activity, 19*, 100357. https://doi.org/10.1016/j.mhpa.2020.100357. https://www.sciencedirect.com/science/article/pii/S1755296620300417

Scherer, A. M., Bruchmann, K., Windtschitl, P. D., Rose, J. P., Smith, A. R., Koestner, B., Snetselaar, L., & Suls, J. (2016). Sources of biases in peoples' social comparative estimates of food consumption. *Journal of Experimental Psychology: Applied, 22*(2), 173–183.

Schwarz, N., Bless, H., Strack, F., Klumpp, G., Rittenauer-Schatka, H., & Simons, A. (1991). Ease of retrieval as information: Another look at the availability heuristic. *Journal of Personality and Social Psychology, 61*(2), 195–202.

Sedikides, C., Gaertner, L., & Toguchi, Y. (2003). Pancultural self-enhancement. *Journal of Personality and Social Psychology, 84*, 60–79.

Seligman, M. (1998). *Learned optimism*. Pocket Books.

Shepperd, J. A., Ouellette, J. A., & Fernandez, J. K. (1996). Abandoning unrealistic optimism: Performance estimates and the temporal proximity of self-relevant feedback. *Journal of Personality and Social Psychology, 70*, 844–855.

Shepperd, J. A., Klein, W. M. P., Waters, E. A., & Weinstein, N. D. (2013). Taking stock of unrealistic optimism. *Perspectives on Psychological Science, 8*(4), 395–411.

Sjastad, H., & Van Bavel, J. (2021). *The best-case heuristic: Relative optimism in a global health pandemic* (Working paper).

Spinney. (2017). *Pale rider: The Spanish flu of 1918 and how it changed the world.*

Sproesser, G., Klusmann, V., Schupp, H. T., & Renner, B. (2017). Self-other differences in perceiving why people eat what they eat. *Frontiers in Psychology, 8*, 209.

Suls, J. M. (1977). Social comparison theory and research. In J. M. Suls & R. M. Miller (Eds.), *Social comparison processes: Theoretical and experimental perspectives* (pp. 1–19). Hemisphere.

Svenson, O. (1981). Are we all less risky and more skillful than our fellow drivers? *Acta Psychologica, 47*, 143–148.

Swann, W. B. (1983). Self-verification: Bringing social reality into harmony with the self. In J. Suls & A. G. Greennwald (Eds.), *Psychological perspectives on the self* (Vol. 2, pp. 33–66). Erlbaum.

Swann, W. B. (1987). Identity negotiation: Where two roads meet. *Journal of Personality and Social Psychology, 53*, 1038–1051.

Swann, W. B., & Read, S. J. (1981). Acquiring self-knowledge: The search for feedback that fits. *Journal of Personality and Social Psychology, 41*, 1119–1128.

Sweeny, K., & Shepperd, J. A. (2010). The costs of optimism and the benefits of pessimism. *Emotion, 10*(5), 750–753.

Taylor, S. E., & Brown, J. D. (1988). Illusion and well-being. A social psychological perspective on mental health. *Psychological Bulletin, 103*, 193–210.

Taylor, S., Landry, C. A., Paluszek, M. M., Fergus, T. A., McKay, D., & Asmundson, G. J. G. (2020). Development and initial validation of the COVID stress scales. *Journal of Anxiety Disorders, 72*, 102232. https://doi.org/10.1016/j.janxdis.2020.102232

Treloar, C., & Hopwood, M. (2008). "Look, I'm fit, I'm positive and I'll be all right, thank you very much": Coping with hepatitis C treatment and unrealistic optimism. *Psychology, Health and Medicine, 13*(3), 360–366.

Trope, Y. (1975). Seeking information about one's own ability as a determinants of choice among tasks. *Journal of Personality and Social Psychology, 32*, 1004–1013.

Tversky, A., & Kahneman, D. (1973). Availability: A heuristic for judging frequency and probability. *Cognitive Psychology, 5*, 207–232.

Tversky, A., & Kahneman, D. (1974). Judgment under uncertainty: Heuristics and biases. *Science, 185*, 1124–1131.

UNESCO. (2021). *When schools shut: Gendered impacts of COVID-19 school closures*. UNESCO.

USAID. (2021). *Preliminary report on COVID-19 research: Data collection and analysis for the early grade reading study (EGRS)*. The reading support project (RSP) and benchmarking. https://pdf.usaid.gov/pdf_docs/PA00XGST.pdf

Van Baaren, R. B., Horgan, T. G., Chartrand, T. L., & Dijkmans, M. (2004). The forest, the trees, and the chameleon: Context dependence and mimicry. *Journal of Personality and Social Psychology, 86*(3), 453–459. https://doi.org/10.1037/0022-3514.86.3.453

Van der Velde, F. W., van der Pligt, J., & Hooykaas, C. (1994). Perceiving AIDS-related risk: Accuracy as a function of differences in actual risk. *Health Psychology, 13*, 25–33.

Van Lange, P. A. M. (1991). Being better but not smarter than others: The Muhammad Ali effect at work in interpersonal situations. *Personality and Social Psychology Bulletin, 17*, 689–693.

Van Lange, P. A. M., & Sedikides, C. (1998). Being more honest but not necessarily more intelligent than others: Generality and explanations for the Muhammad Ali effect. *European Journal of Social Psychology, 28*, 675–680.

Van Swol, L. M., & Drury-Grogan, M. L. (2017). The effects of shared opinions on nonverbal mimicry. *SAGE Open, 7*(2), 215824401770724. https://doi.org/10.1177/2158244017707243

Vanderlind, W. M., Rabinovitz, B. B., Miao, I. Y., Oberlin, L. E., Bueno-Castellano, C., Fridman, C., et al. (2021). A systematic review of neuropsychological and psychiatric sequelae of COVID-19: Implications for treatment. *Current Opinion in Psychiatry, 34*(4), 420–433. https://doi.org/10.1097/YCO.0000000000000713

Vieites, Y., Ramos, G. A., Pereira, A. C., & Medeiros, A. (2021). Can self-protective behaviors increase unrealistic optimism? Evidence from the COVID-19 pandemic. *Journal of Experimental Psychology: Applied, 27*(4), 621–631.

Virhammar, J., Kumlien, E., Fällmar, D., Frithiof, R., Jackmann, S., Sköld, M. K., et al. (2020). Acute necrotizing encephalopathy with SARS-CoV-2 RNA confirmed in cerebrospinal fluid. *Neurology, 95*(10), 445–449. https://doi.org/10.1212/WNL.0000000000010250

Wang, X., Hegde, S., Son, C., Keller, B., Smith, A., & Sasangohar, F. (2020). Investigating mental health of US college students during the COVID-19 pandemic: Cross-sectional survey study. *Journal of Medical Internet Research, 22*(9), e22817. https://doi.org/10.2196/22817

Weinstein, N. D. (1980). Unrealistic optimism about future life events. *Journal of Personality and Social Psychology, 39*(5), 806–820.

Weinstein, N. D. (1983). Reducing unrealistic optimism about illness susceptibility. *Health Psychology, 2*(1), 11–20.

Weinstein, N. D. (1984). Why it won't happen to me: Perceptions of risk factors and susceptibility. *Health Psychology, 3*(5), 431–457.

Weinstein, N. D. (1987). Unrealistic optimism about susceptibility to health problems: Conclusions from a community-wide sample. *Journal of Behavioral Medicine, 10*, 481–500.

Weinstein, N. D., & Lachendro, E. (1982). Egocentrism as a source of unrealistic optimism. *Personality and Social Psychology Bulletin, 8*, 195–200.

Weiss, J. W., & Garbanati, J. A. (2006). Effects of acculturation and social norms on adolescent smoking among Asian-American subgroups. *Journal of Ethnicity in Substance Abuse, 5*(2), 75–90.

Wills, T. A. (1981). Downward comparison principles in social psychology. *Psychological Bulletin, 90*, 245–271.

Wills, T. A. (1987). Downward comparison as a coping mechanism. In C. R. Snyder & C. Ford (Eds.), *Coping with negative life events* (pp. 243–268). Plenum Press.

Wise, T., Zbozinek, T. D., Michelini, G., Hagan, C. C., & Mobbs, D. (2020). Changes in risk perception and self-reported protective behaviour during the first week of the COVID-19 pandemic in the United States. *Royal Society Open Science, 7*, 200742.

Woo, M. S., Malsy, J., Pöttgen, J., Seddiq Zai, S., Ufer, F., Hadjilaou, A., et al. (2020). Frequent neurocognitive deficits after recovery from mild COVID-19. *Brain Communications, 2*(2), fcaa205. https://doi.org/10.1093/braincomms/fcaa205

Yang, S., Markoczy, L., & Qi, M. (2007). Unrealistic optimism in consumer credit card adoption. *Journal of Economic Psychology, 28*(2), 170–185.

Yong, S. J. (2021). Persistent brainstem dysfunction in long-COVID: A hypothesis. *ACS Chemical Neuroscience, 12*(4), 573–580. https://doi.org/10.1021/acschemneuro.0c00793

Young, M. C. (2014). Do positive illusions contribute to human well-being? *Philosophical Psychology, 27*, 536–552.

Young-Hoon, K., & Chi-Yue, C. (2011). Emotional cost of inaccurate self-assessments: Both self-effacement and self-enhancement can lead to dejection. *Emotion, 11*(5), 1096–1104.

Yuan, Y., Liu, Z. H., Zhao, Y. J., Zhang, Q., Zhang, L., Cheung, T., et al. (2021). Prevalence of post-traumatic stress symptoms and its associations with quality of life, demographic and clinical characteristics in COVID-19 survivors during the post-COVID-19 era. *Frontiers in Psychiatry, 12*, 665507.

Zandersen, M., & Parnas, J. (2019). Identity disturbance, feeling of emptiness and the boundaries of the schizophrenia spectrum. *Schizophrenia Bulletin, 45*, 106–113.

Zell, E., Strickouser, J. E., Sedikides, C., & Alicke, M. D. (2020). The better-than-average effect in comparative self-evaluation: A comprehensive review and meta-analysis. *Psychological Bulletin, 156*(2), 118–149.

Ziano, I., Mok, P.Y. (Cora), & Feldman, G. (2020). Replication and extension of Alicke (1985) better-than-average effect for desirable and controllable traits. *Social Psychological and Personality Science, 12*(6), 1005–1017.

Zoghi, A., Ramezani, M., Roozbeh, M., Darazam, I. A., & Sahraian, M. (2020). A case of possible atypical demyelinating event of the central nervous system following COVID-19. *Multiple Sclerosis and Related Disorders, 44*, 102324. https://doi.org/10.1016/j.msard.2020.102324

Index

W. Kulesza, D. Doliński, *Social Biases During Covid 19*, SpringerBriefs in Psychology, https://doi.org/10.1007/978-3-031-34706-1

M

N

O

P

R

S

T

U

W

Printed by Printforce, the Netherlands